DATE DUE

ILL Dec 2014

TEEN RIGHTS AND FREEDOMS

| Education

TEEN RIGHTS AND FREEDOMS

| Education

Christina Fisanick
Book Editor

GREENHAVEN PRESS
A part of Gale, Cengage Learning

GALE
CENGAGE Learning·

Detroit • New York • San Francisco • New Haven, Conn • Waterville, Maine • London

Elizabeth Des Chenes, *Managing Editor*

© 2012 Greenhaven Press, a part of Gale, Cengage Learning

For more information, contact:
Greenhaven Press
27500 Drake Rd.
Farmington Hills, MI 48331-3535
Or you can visit our Internet site at gale.cengage.com.

For product information and technology assistance, contact us at:

Gale Customer Support, 1-800-877-4253.
For permission to use material from this text or product, submit all requests online at www.cengage.com/permissions.

Further permissions questions can be emailed to permissionrequest@cengage.com.

Articles in Greenhaven Press anthologies are often edited for length to meet page requirements. In addition, original titles of these works are changed to clearly present the main thesis and to explicitly indicate the author's opinion. Every effort is made to ensure the Greenhaven Press accurately reflects the original intent of the authors. Every effort has been made to trace the owners of copyrighted material.

Cover Image © l i g h t p o e t / Shutterstock.com.

LIBRARY OF CONGRESS CATALOGING-IN-PUBLICATION DATA

Education / Christina Fisanick, book editor.
    p. cm. -- (Teen rights and freedoms)
    Includes bibliographical references and index.
    ISBN 978-0-7377-5824-5 (hardcover)
 1. Educational law and legislation--United States--Cases. 2. Constitutional law--United States--Cases. I. Fisanick, Christina.
    KF4119.E268 2012
    344.73'071--dc23

                                                            2011029276

Printed in the United States of America
1 2 3 4 5 6 7 15 14 13 12 11

Contents

Nearly forty years after the landmark Supreme Court case, Mary Beth Tinker reflects on the impact of the decision and the current state of student rights.

William Rehnquist

The *Hendrick Hudson Board of Education v. Rowley* decision states that all public school students, including children with disabilities, have the right to a quality education, but not if the services needed exceed the capabilities of the school system. The school system need only to provide services and tools necessary for appropriate educational access.

Amy June Rowley

Twenty-five years after the decision of *Hendrick v. Rowley*, the woman at the center of the case reflects on her experiences as a child caught up in the drama of a Supreme Court case. Rowley also offers her assessment of the state of education for children with disabilities today.

William Brennan

The *Plyler v. Doe* decision indicates that states cannot deny public school funding to children of illegal immigrants.

Sex education programs that advocate abstinence-only behavior by teens until they are married put youngsters at risk by providing inaccurate and inadequate information, and by perpetuating harmful stereotypes. Furthermore, they often violate the US Constitution by using federal funding to put forth religious views.

Foreword

*"In the truest sense freedom cannot be
bestowed, it must be achieved."*
          Franklin D. Roosevelt,
          September 16, 1936

The notion of children and teens having rights is a relatively recent development. Early in American history, the head of the household—nearly always the father—exercised complete control over the children in the family. Children were legally considered to be the property of their parents. Over time, this view changed, as society began to acknowledge that children have rights independent of their parents, and that the law should protect young people from exploitation. By the early twentieth century, more and more social reformers focused on the welfare of children, and over the ensuing decades advocates worked to protect them from harm in the workplace, to secure public education for all, and to guarantee fair treatment for youths in the criminal justice system. Throughout the twentieth century, rights for children and teens—and restrictions on those rights—were established by Congress and reinforced by the courts. Today's courts are still defining and clarifying the rights and freedoms of young people, sometimes expanding those rights and sometimes limiting them. Some teen rights are outside the scope of public law and remain in the realm of the family, while still others are determined by school policies.

Each volume in the Teen Rights and Freedoms series focuses on a different right or freedom and offers an anthology of key essays and articles on that right or freedom and the responsibilities that come with it. Material within each volume is drawn from a diverse selection of primary and secondary sources— journals, magazines, newspapers, nonfiction books, organization newsletters, position papers, speeches, and government documents, with a particular emphasis on Supreme Court and lower court decisions. Volumes also include first-person narratives from young people and others involved in teen rights issues, such as parents and educators. The material is selected and arranged to highlight all the major social and legal controversies relating to the right or freedom under discussion. Each selection is preceded by an introduction that provides context and background. In many cases, the essays point to the difference between adult and teen rights, and why this difference exists.

Many of the volumes cover rights guaranteed under the Bill of Rights and how these rights are interpreted and protected in regard to children and teens, including freedom of speech, freedom of the press, due process, and religious rights. The scope of the series also encompasses rights or freedoms, whether real or perceived, relating to the school environment, such as electronic devices, dress, Internet policies, and privacy. Some volumes focus on the home environment, including topics such as parental control and sexuality.

Numerous features are included in each volume of Teen Rights and Freedoms:

- An annotated **table of contents** provides a brief summary of each essay in the volume and highlights court decisions and personal narratives.

- An **introduction** specific to the volume topic gives context for the right or freedom and its impact on daily life.

- A brief **chronology** offers important dates associated with the right or freedom, including landmark court cases.

- **Primary sources**—including personal narratives and court decisions—are among the varied selections in the anthology.

- **Illustrations**—including photographs, charts, graphs, tables, statistics, and maps—are closely tied to the text and chosen to help readers understand key points or concepts.

- An annotated list of **organizations to contact** presents sources of additional information on the topic.

- A **for further reading** section offers a bibliography of books, periodical articles, and Internet sources for further research.

- A comprehensive subject **index** provides access to key people, places, events, and subjects cited in the text.

Each volume of Teen Rights and Freedoms delves deeply into the issues most relevant to the lives of teens: their own rights, freedoms, and responsibilities. With the help of this series, students and other readers can explore from many angles the evolution and current expression of rights both historic and contemporary.

Introduction

"Today, it would be most accurate to say that public school students have some First Amendment rights in schools, but certainly not as many as adults do in the real world."

Encyclopedia of Everyday Law,
2011

Over the past several decades, the US Supreme Court has ruled on a variety of cases involving student rights and freedoms. From racial equality to religious freedom to equal access for disabled students, the Court has made a number of decisions that have changed the face of American education. Many of the cases in the past fifty years have focused on students' free speech rights. Not all decisions have been in favor of students, however, as was the situation in the 2007 case informally referred to as "Bong Hits 4 Jesus."

In a landmark 1969 case, the Supreme Court ruled in favor of student free speech rights in *Tinker v. Des Moines Independent Community School District.* In December 1965, three students wore black armbands to school to support a nationwide protest of the Vietnam War. School officials enacted a policy that prohibited armbands being worn at school, with the punishment being suspension until the students removed the bands. John Tinker, his sister Mary Beth Tinker, and their friend Christopher Eckhardt were suspended and did not return until after the protest was over. They sued the school district for violation of free speech. The case went as far as the Supreme Court, which decided in favor of the students, arguing that wearing the black armbands was a form of speech guaranteed under the First Amendment.

The *Tinker* ruling is significant in terms of student rights. Not only did the justices create a method for determining future freedom of speech cases for students, now known as the *Tinker* Test, but they also issued a statement that has been the rallying cry for advocates of free student expression ever since. The Court asserted, "It can hardly be argued that either students or teachers shed their constitutional rights to freedom of speech or expression at the schoolhouse gate."

In 2002 Joseph Frederick, a student in Juneau, Alaska, was suspended from school after displaying a sign reading "Bong Hits 4 Jesus" on the sidewalk across from his school during an Olympic Torch rally. His high school principal, Deborah Morse, defended her decision by arguing that the banner supported illegal drug use, which is against school policy. Ultimately, the Court ruled in favor of Morse, noting that the school had a right to suspend Frederick because he was in attendance at a school event and the banner promotes smoking marijuana, which is against school rules.

The justices had to decide on three issues in the case. First, they had to determine if indeed the student was violating school policy, given that he was not on official school grounds. Frederick argued that he was on the sidewalk across from the school. However, Chief Justice John Roberts stated, "We agree with the superintendent that Frederick cannot 'stand in the midst of his fellow students, during school hours, at a school-sanctioned activity and claim he is not at school.'"

In addition, the justices had to decide if Frederick's banner advocated the use of illegal drugs. Although some justices felt that Frederick's banner was simply a ploy to get attention, in which case his actions would be protected, the majority insisted that the implications of "Bong Hits 4 Jesus" is the encouragement of illegal drug use. In addition, Justice Roberts notes, "not even Frederick argues that the banner conveys any sort of political or religious message." Therefore, Roberts concludes, "this is plainly not a case about political debate over the criminalization of drug use or possession."

Finally, the justices had to determine if school principals have the right to restrict student speech. Roberts cited several previous court cases that demonstrate principal rights, including *Bethel School District No. 403 v. Fraser* (1986) and *Hazelwood School District v. Kuhlmeier* (1988). In the *Bethel* case, it was decided that school officials have the right to restrict student speech if it disrupts the education of others. The *Hazelwood* ruling found in favor of school officials controlling student journalism when the forum in question is part of the school curriculum. Using those rulings, Roberts concludes, "Principal Morse's failure to act against the banner would send a powerful message to the students in her charge, including Frederick, about how serious the school was about the dangers of illegal drug use." The First Amendment does not protect against speech acts that could put other students in harm's way. In their final decision, the justices found in favor of Principal Morse.

Since the Court's ruling was made official in 2007, a number of people have spoken out about the case. In addition to free speech scholars, Mary Beth Tinker attended the Supreme Court hearings in support of Frederick. In a March 19, 2007, interview with the American Civil Liberties Union (ACLU), Tinker said, "Students have a lot to speak out about, and they are the natural ones to do it. That's what our democracy is all about—that the ones affected should have a say." In addition to the ACLU and Tinker, Frederick had the backing of the American Center for Law and Justice, the Christian Legal Society, the Rutherford Institute, the Student Press Law Center, Lambda Legal Defense and Education Fund, the Drug Policy Alliance, and the National Coalition Against Censorship.

A number of individuals and organizations, however, found Principal Morse's action and thereby the Court's decision to be fair, including the National School Boards Association. In her opinion of the case in a March 22, 2007, article on FindLaw.com, Yeshiva University law professor Marci Hamilton argues that if the judges would have found in favor of Frederick, then it would have weakened support of student rights to free speech. She argues, "To protect this nonsense speech actually devalues the *Tinker* Court's ruling in favor of serious political speech."

In *Teen Rights and Freedoms: Education*, the authors present a variety of viewpoints on this decidedly divisive subject and many others involving the education of America's young people. Among other topics, the authors debate the right to religious expression in schools, the rights of disabled students in the classroom, and the role of Title IX in protecting pregnant students. In the end, it is clear that teens can be advocates for change as they work alongside adult supporters who wish to protect their best interests.

Chronology

1943　　　The Supreme Court issues its opinion in *West Virginia State Board of Education v. Barnette*, arguing that the Free Speech Clause in the First Amendment made it unconstitutional for students to be required to salute the American flag or say the Pledge of Allegiance.

1954　　　The Supreme Court declares in *Brown v. the Board of Education of Topeka, Kansas*, that state laws establishing "separate, but equal" public schools for black and white students are unconstitutional.

1962　　　The Supreme Court rules in *Engel v. Vitale*, arguing that states cannot require public school students to pray in school.

1969　　　The Supreme Court issues its opinion in *Tinker v. Des Moines Independent Community School District*, defining students' free speech rights by finding in favor of students who wore armbands to school to protest the Vietnam War.

1972　　　Title IX passes into law and guarantees the right to a federally funded education regardless of gender.

1974　　　The Family Educational Rights and Privacy Act of 1974 (FERPA) is signed into law, giving parents and eligible students the right to inspect, review, and amend their educational records.

1975 The Supreme Court states in *Goss v. Lopez* that suspending students without a hearing violates the Due Process Clause of the Fourteenth Amendment.

1982 The Supreme Court issues its opinion in *Hazelwood v. Kuhlmeier*, stating that school administrators have final say over public school student newspapers that are part of the curriculum and not an independent forum for student expression.

1985 The Supreme Court rules in *New Jersey v. T.L.O.* that the search of a student who was caught smoking did not violate her Fourth Amendment rights against unreasonable searches.

1987 The Supreme Court states in *Bethel School District No. 43 v. Fraser* that obscene speech made by students is not upheld by the First Amendment right to free speech.

2000 The Supreme Court issues its opinion in *Santa Fe Independent School District v. Doe*, arguing that student-led student prayers at football games violate the Establishment Clause of the First Amendment.

2002   The Supreme Court issues its opinion in *Board of Education of Independent School District No. 92 of Pottawatomie County v. Earls*, allowing for students who participate in extracurricular activities to be drug tested.

2002   The Supreme Court states in *Zelma v. Simmons-Harris* that the Ohio school voucher program, which provides the opportunity for students in the Cleveland City School District to attend any public or private school of their choosing, does not violate the Establishment Clause of the First Amendment.

2007   The Supreme Court rules in *Morse and the Juneau School Board et al. v. Frederick* that student speech at school events is not protected by the First Amendment if the speech in question advocates illegal drug use.

> *"Students can invoke their constitutional rights to preserve personal liberties and to ensure equal treatment."*

Education and the Constitution: An Overview

Betsy Levin

Betsy Levin specializes in educational law and is a law professor at Chapman University in California. In the following viewpoint she provides an overview of students' rights and the US Constitution. Beginning with the Pierce *compromise (1925) and ending with the current state of immigrant education, Levin traces the evolution of teen rights and freedoms in the educational realm through major Supreme Court decisions.*

Because education plays such an important part in children's development, the Constitution affords significant protections against government overreaching and abuse. Students can invoke their constitutional rights to preserve personal liberties and to ensure equal treatment. The free speech clause provides a basis for challenging practices that censor unpopular or controversial views. Moreover, equal protection enables students to contest one-size-fits-all policies that disregard individual differences. In resolving these disputes, federal courts must balance the schools' desire for control and standardization with the students' demands for autonomy and non-discrimination. . . .

Compulsory Education and the *Pierce* Compromise

In the earliest years of the American republic, public schooling was quite rudimentary. In a rural, agrarian economy, only minimal formal education was necessary for individuals to become productive adults. As the United States became an increasingly urban and industrialized nation, the need for a consolidated system of schooling grew. States developed public school systems to ensure that there would be a qualified workforce and informed citizenry. As these systems were professionalized and bureaucratized, states enacted compulsory education laws and vigorously enforced them. Truant pupils could be forced to go to class, and parents could be subject to criminal penalties for failing to ensure that their children went to school. Compulsory education laws made clear that the government would exercise significant authority over a child's development, sometimes in contravention of parents' wishes.

Tensions over who had primary authority to direct children's schooling came to a head in the early 1900s. During World War I (1914–1918), fears of foreign influence led to concerns that some immigrant parents would not instill patriotic American values in their children. To counter this perceived danger, Oregon voters passed a popular initiative in 1922 that mandated that all students attend public schools where they could be "Americanized." The legislation was largely aimed at shutting down Catholic schools, a tactic that the *Portland Telegram* (Nov. 1, 1922) described as "religious revenge." Two private schools, one secular and one sectarian, challenged the law as an infringement on educators' rights to pursue their livelihood. In addition, although no parents or students came forward to sue, presumably out of fear of reprisal, the two schools also argued that the provision violated parents' rights to bring up children as they saw fit.

In *Pierce v. Society of Sisters* (1925), the Court crafted what has come to be called the *Pierce* compromise. The justices found Oregon's law violated due process because compelling attendance exclusively at public schools was unduly authoritarian and undermined personal freedoms. To preserve institutional and parental autonomy, families must have the option to send children to private institutions that would reflect distinct values and goals. The decision was a compromise, however, because parents still had to pay taxes to support public education and could opt for private schooling only if they had the means to afford it.

 ## The Right to Education

1. Everyone has the right to education. Education shall be free, at least in the elementary and fundamental stages. Elementary education shall be compulsory. Technical and professional education shall be made generally available and higher education shall be equally accessible to all on the basis of merit.

2. Education shall be directed to the full development of the human personality and to the strengthening of respect for human rights and fundamental freedoms. It shall promote understanding, tolerance and friendship among all nations, racial or religious groups, and shall further the activities of the United Nations for the maintenance of peace.

3. Parents have a prior right to choose the kind of education that shall be given to their children.

United Nations, "Universal Declaration of Human Rights," Article 26, General Assembly Resolution 217 (III), December 10, 1948.

Moreover, private schools remained subject to reasonable regulation of their operations, including hours and days of instruction, basic curriculum, facilities, and teacher qualifications.

The *Pierce* compromise recognized rights nowhere mentioned in the Constitution by relying on "substantive due process." This doctrine came under attack as an unwarranted form of judicial activism that permitted rights to be made out of whole cloth. As a result, some legal scholars questioned *Pierce*'s ongoing vitality. Any doubts about the constitutional status of parental rights were laid to rest when the Court decided *Wisconsin v. Yoder* (1972). [In that case], the Court addressed a Wisconsin law that required children to attend public or private school until age sixteen. The Amish were willing to send their children to public school until they were fourteen, but after that, young people were expected to immerse themselves in the life of the community. Youth would learn by doing and be shielded from worldly influences found in high school. The Court concluded that Wisconsin lacked a sufficiently compelling reason to force students to go to two years of high school, particularly when attendance conflicted with an interest in the free exercise of religion and the right to bring up children as parents saw fit.

Student Liberties and the First Amendment

Although the *Pierce* compromise remains robust, most students still attend public school. To prepare children for work and civic life, educators rely not only on a formal curriculum of academic subjects but also on an informal curriculum of good conduct. Students must show up on time, remain obedient and orderly in the classroom, and behave themselves in the cafeteria and on the playground. In some cases, students complain that disciplinary sanctions are nothing but coercion and censorship. For instance, in *West Virginia State Board of Education v. Barnette* (1943), public school pupils began the day by saluting the flag and saying the Pledge of Allegiance. Students who refused to participate were

expelled for insubordination. Jehovah's Witnesses
their children could not bow down to any graven in
ing the flag. Although the parents emphasized the l
posed on children because of their religion, the just
on the coerced nature of the oath of allegiance. In finding a First
Amendment violation, the Court concluded that: "If there is any
fixed star in our constitutional constellation, it is that no official,
high or petty, can prescribe what shall be orthodox in politics,
nationalism, religion, or other matters of opinion or force citizens to confess by word or act their faith therein."

In *Tinker v. Des Moines School District* (1969), three pupils
wore black armbands to their public junior high and high schools
to protest American involvement in the Vietnam War. Each was
sent home and suspended. The students challenged their suspensions on free speech grounds. Again, the Court found a First
Amendment violation. The justices first noted that neither teachers nor students "shed their constitutional rights to freedom of
speech or expression at the schoolhouse gate." The armbands
amounted to speech because they sent a symbolic message of
protest. The suspensions were unjustified because there was no
evidence that the armbands had led to any problems other than
a few hostile remarks from peers outside the classroom. School
administrators had acted out of a mere fear of controversy, but
the Constitution required more. To silence the students, officials
had to show that the speech threatened "a substantial disruption
of or material interference with school activities."

Tinker set a high standard for censoring student expression
on public school grounds. Later, however, the Court seemed to
retreat from this position. In *Bethel School District No. 403 v.
Fraser* (1986), Matthew Fraser, a public high school pupil, used
"an elaborate, graphic, and explicit sexual metaphor" in nomi-
nating a candidate for student body vice president at an assembly. During the speech, some classmates in the audience hooted,
yelled, and used gestures to simulate sexual activity. Afterward,
Fraser was suspended and denied the chance to be considered as

graduation speaker for violating a rule that prohibited, among other things, "the use of obscene, profane language or gestures" when they "materially and substantially interfere with the educational process." Fraser challenged the punishment as a violation of his free speech rights.

In finding for *Fraser*, the lower courts concluded that his speech was indistinguishable from that in *Tinker* because neither threatened serious interference with school activities. The Supreme Court disagreed because it found that the school had an interest in inculcating "habits and manners of civility" at school functions. Consequently, Fraser could be punished for using "pervasive sexual innuendo" that "was plainly offensive to both teachers and students." The Court again distinguished *Tinker* when it upheld a public high school principal's right to delete articles in a student paper. Because the school sponsored the paper, the justices required only a reasonable basis for censoring the material based on sound pedagogical objectives (*Hazelwood School District v. Kuhlmeier* [1988]).

In some cases, students have asserted that public schools did not properly draw the line between church and state. Under the First Amendment's establishment clause, the government must remain neutral with respect to religion. State officials cannot prefer one religion to another, nor can they prefer religion to irreligion. As a result, the Court has refused to allow public school-teachers to lead students in prayer (*Abington School District v. Schempp* [1963]). As an alternative, some state legislatures have enacted "moment of silence" statutes. In Alabama, the law authorized a one-minute period of silence for meditation or voluntary prayer. The father of three young elementary school students complained that teachers were using the statute to engage in religious indoctrination when teachers led their classes in prayer. The Court concluded that a moment of silence law might be constitutional in theory, but Alabama's statute had been amended over the years with "the sole purpose of expressing the State's endorsement of prayer activities." As a result, the law violated the government's obligation of neutrality in ways that curtailed "the individual's freedom to believe, to worship, and to express himself in accordance with the dictates of his own conscience" (*Wallace v. Jaffree* [1985]). Later, the Court held that prayers at public school graduation ceremonies and football games have similarly coercive effects (*Lee v. Weisman* [1992]; *Santa Fe Independent School District v. Doe* [2000]).

In response to the Court's rulings, students increasingly turned to religious activities that they initiated themselves. Some public high schools denied pupils permission to form sectarian clubs out of concern that they would violate a principle of neutrality. Students insisted that the denial was impermissible discrimination; that is, applications were treated differently based on whether members would adopt a religious or secular viewpoint. This discrimination claim has met with some success, though on nonconstitutional grounds. In 1984, Congress enacted the Equal Access Act to protect the rights of public secondary students to form organizations. The Act prohibits schools that recognize some clubs from discriminating against others on the basis of "religious, political, philosophical, or other content of the speech at such meetings." The Court upheld the Act, finding that it did not violate the schools' obligation of religious neutrality, and used the provisions to protect the rights of students who wanted to form a Christian club. The justices did not decide whether students, in the absence of the Act, would have an independent constitutional right to organize the club (*Board of Education of Westside Community Schools v. Mergens* [1990]).

Equality and the Fourteenth Amendment

When religious students challenge school policies as discriminatory, they are building on a long history of invoking equal protection under the Fourteenth Amendment to ensure that schools fully include children regardless of race, ethnicity, gender, or national origin. The cornerstone of equality jurisprudence is

Brown v. Board of Education (1954). There, black students successfully argued that official policies of racial segregation in public schools were unconstitutional. The Court concluded that "[s]eparate educational facilities are inherently unequal" because they stigmatize black children by generating "a feeling of inferiority as to their status in the community that may affect their hearts and minds in a way unlikely ever to be undone." After a substantial period of delay, Congress backed up the *Brown* decision with civil rights laws and vigorous enforcement efforts. School districts guilty of mandating segregation by law had to eliminate the vestiges "root and branch" by, among other things, reconfiguring attendance zones, reassigning faculty and staff, and busing students to schools outside their neighborhoods (*Green v. County School Board* [1968]; *Swann v. Charlotte-Mecklenburg Board of Education* [1971]). Integration became part of a strategy to enable blacks to assimilate fully into American society.

Brown and its aftermath inspired other groups to consider whether they were receiving an equal educational opportunity. For instance, girls had been excluded from all-male academies, denied the opportunity to participate in all-male sports programs, and sent to special classes for pregnant students and teenage mothers. Gender complicated equality claims because sex segregation was not rooted in the same invidious history as racial segregation. As a result, two schools of thought emerged. Sameness theorists claimed that equality requires a process of assimilation so that girls and boys enjoy identical opportunities. Under this view, for instance, girls should be allowed to try out for a football squad; even if most would not make the team, each would have a chance to show that she could meet the same standard as boys do (e.g., *Force v. Pierce City R-VI School District* [1983]). Difference theorists argued that there is value in respecting the fact that girls and boys are not the same. Equality should mean that males and females have equivalent, though not necessarily identical, opportunities. Under this view, girls would have access to sports programs, but these could be teams designed especially for them, so long as the programs for males and females received comparable support.

In 1972, Congress passed Title IX to resolve some of the dis-agreements about what gender equality means. Even so, these issues continue to divide the courts. With respect to pregnancy, judges generally have held that public schools can maintain sep-arate programs for pregnant teenagers and teenage mothers so long as participation is voluntary and instruction is comparable to that in other classes. However, courts have split over whether pregnant students can be expelled from honorary societies. Some decisions have concluded that the practice amounts to discrimi-nation because males who impregnate a classmate are not sim-ilarly punished (e.g., *Chipman v. Grant County School District* [1998]). Other cases have found that there is no discrimination because female students are expelled for failing to meet standards of high moral conduct, rather than for being pregnant (*Pfeiffer v. Marion Center Area School District* [3d Cir. 1990]).

Amid the debate over what equality means, the United States Supreme Court has spoken most clearly to the constitutional-ity of single-sex education. In *United States v. Virginia* (1996), the Court struck down a males-only admissions policy at the Virginia Military Institute (VMI), an elite public institution. VMI argued that admitting females would undermine its adversative method of instruction, which was designed to prepare students for careers in the armed services through endurance of physical hardship and psychological stress. Adopting the approach advo-cated by sameness theorists, the Court found that VMI could not deny those females who would benefit from its instructional pro-gram the opportunity to apply. Even though many women would not be interested ([likewise,] many men would not be), Virginia had not offered an "exceedingly persuasive justification" for fore-closing "women who want a VMI education and can make the grade" from competing for admission.

Race and gender have garnered the most significant constitu-tional protection, but Congress has drawn on these examples to

The passage of Title IX in 1972 was designed to allow for greater opportunities for girls in education, including sports programs and admission to prestigious military academies. © Kevin Clark/The Washington Post/Getty Images.

protect other vulnerable groups under federal anti-discrimination laws. Under the Individuals with Disabilities in Education Act, public schools cannot discriminate against students with disabilities, and officials must prepare individualized educational plans to ensure adequate access to the curriculum. Because of the substantial expense involved in accommodating students' special needs, parents and schools regularly litigate over whether plans are appropriate. In fact, disability lawsuits have grown to be among the most common that school districts face.

Congress also has passed provisions to protect students who speak a language other than English. In *Lau v. Nichols* (1974), the Court upheld the Office for Civil Rights' efforts to protect language minority students under Title VI of the Civil Rights Act. The Court agreed that the statute required school districts to take affirmative steps to address language barriers when they effectively denied students access to the curriculum—at least where language served as a proxy for race, ethnicity, or national origin. *Lau* did not mandate any particular form of instruction. Later, when Congress codified *Lau* by enacting the Equal Educational Opportunities Act of 1974, the law again failed to specify particular remedies. Because Congress and the Court have been agnostic [noncommittal] about educational methods, debates persist over whether schools should use intensive English instruction or bilingual programs that incorporate a child's native language. Proponents of intensive English instruction see this approach as a rapid route to full assimilation, while advocates of bilingual programs insist that [the method they support] demonstrates respect for linguistic and cultural difference. . . .

Clearly, the Constitution plays an important role in striking a balance between the prerogatives of government and the rights of individuals. The Court has struggled to preserve public educators' discretion to implement programs and activities, without overlooking the dangers of marginalization that confront students who refuse to conform or have special needs. The problems are sufficiently subtle and the stakes sufficiently high that the Court undoubtedly will grapple with questions of liberty and equality in the public schools for years to come.

"We conclude that in the field of public education the doctrine of 'separate but equal' has no place."

Separate Accommodations for African American Students Are Not Equal

The Supreme Court's Decision

Earl Warren

Brown v. the Board of Education of Topeka, Kansas, *is a Supreme Court case that consolidated several cases from Kansas, South Carolina, Virginia, and Delaware. Lawyers on behalf of African American children sued so that the children could be admitted to public schools that required or permitted segregation based on race. The plaintiffs alleged that segregation based on race is unconstitutional under the Equal Protection Clause of the Fourteenth Amendment. In addition, they argued that schools designated for black children, even those with similar facilities, would never be equal to white schools. In other words, the plaintiffs argued for the overturning of the ruling* Plessy v. Ferguson *(1896), which made it legal to segregate if separate but equal facilities are provided. Ultimately, the justices in* Brown v. Board, *led by Chief Justice Earl*

Earl Warren, Majority opinion, *Brown v. the Board of Education of Topeka, Kansas*, US Supreme Court, May 17, 1954. Copyright © 1954 The Supreme Court of the United States.

Warren, ruled that all children, regardless of race, have the right to an equal education under the Constitution, and that segregation prevents that equality. Earl Warren served as Chief Justice of the Supreme Court from 1953 to 1969.

Segregation of white and Negro children in the public schools of a State solely on the basis of race, pursuant to state laws permitting or requiring such segregation, denies to Negro children the equal protection of the laws guaranteed by the Fourteenth Amendment—even though the physical facilities and other "tangible" factors of white and Negro schools may be equal.

(a) The history of the Fourteenth Amendment is inconclusive as to its intended effect on public education.

(b) The question presented in these cases must be determined, not on the basis of conditions existing when the Fourteenth Amendment was adopted, but in the light of the full development of public education and its present place in American life throughout the Nation.

(c) Where a State has undertaken to provide an opportunity for an education in its public schools, such an opportunity is a right which must be made available to all on equal terms.

(d) Segregation of children in public schools solely on the basis of race deprives children of the minority group of equal educational opportunities, even though the physical facilities and other "tangible" factors may be equal.

(e) The "separate but equal" doctrine adopted in *Plessy v. Ferguson* has no place in the field of public education. . . .

The Fourteenth Amendment

These cases come to us from the States of Kansas, South Carolina, Virginia, and Delaware. They are premised on different facts and different local conditions, but a common legal question justifies their consideration together in this consolidated opinion.

In each of the cases, minors of the Negro race, through their legal representatives, seek the aid of the courts in obtaining admission to the public schools of their community on a nonsegregated basis. In each instance, they had been denied admission to schools attended by white children under laws requiring or permitting segregation according to race. This segregation was alleged to deprive the plaintiffs of the equal protection of the laws under the Fourteenth Amendment. In each of the cases other than the Delaware case, a three-judge federal district court denied relief to the plaintiffs on the so-called "separate but equal" doctrine announced by this Court in *Plessy v. Ferguson*. Under that doctrine, equality of treatment is accorded when the races are provided substantially equal facilities, even though these facilities be separate. In the Delaware case, the Supreme Court of Delaware adhered to that doctrine, but ordered that the plaintiffs be admitted to the white schools because of their superiority to the Negro schools.

The plaintiffs contend that segregated public schools are not "equal" and cannot be made "equal," and that hence they are deprived of the equal protection of the laws. Because of the obvious importance of the question presented, the Court took jurisdiction. Argument was heard in the 1952 Term, and reargument was heard this Term on certain questions propounded by the Court.

Reargument was largely devoted to the circumstances surrounding the adoption of the Fourteenth Amendment in 1868. It covered exhaustively consideration of the Amendment in Congress, ratification by the states, then-existing practices in racial segregation, and the views of proponents and opponents of the Amendment. This discussion and our own investigation convince us that, although these sources cast some light, it is not enough to resolve the problem with which we are faced. At best, they are inconclusive. The most avid proponents of the post-War Amendments undoubtedly intended them to remove all legal distinctions among "all persons born or naturalized in

The Due Process Clause of the Fourteenth Amendment

Section. 1. All persons born or naturalized in the United States and subject to the jurisdiction thereof, are citizens of the United States and of the State wherein they reside. No State shall make or enforce any law which shall abridge the privileges or immunities of citizens of the United States; nor shall any State deprive any person of life, liberty, or property, without due process of law; nor deny to any person within its jurisdiction the equal protection of the laws.

Fourteenth Amendment, US Constitution.
Adopted July 9, 1868.

the United States." Their opponents, just as certainly, were antagonistic to both the letter and the spirit of the Amendments and wished them to have the most limited effect. What others in Congress and the state legislatures had in mind cannot be determined with any degree of certainty.

An additional reason for the inconclusive nature of the Amendment's history, with respect to segregated schools, is the status of public education at that time. In the South, the movement toward free common schools, supported by general taxation, had not yet taken hold. Education of white children was largely in the hands of private groups. Education of Negroes was almost nonexistent, and practically all of the race were illiterate. In fact, any education of Negroes was forbidden by law in some states. Today, in contrast, many Negroes have achieved outstanding success in the arts and sciences as well as in the business and professional world. It is true that public school education at the time of the Amendment had advanced further in the North, but the effect of the Amendment on Northern States

Linda Brown (front, center) sits in a segregated classroom at the Monroe School in 1953 before the case on her behalf was brought before the Supreme Court. © Carl Iwasaki/Time & Life Pictures/Getty Images.

was generally ignored in the congressional debates. Even in the North, the conditions of public education did not approximate those existing today. The curriculum was usually rudimentary; ungraded schools were common in rural areas; the school term was but three months a year in many states; and compulsory school attendance was virtually unknown. As a consequence, it is not surprising that there should be so little in the history of the Fourteenth Amendment relating to its intended effect on public education.

In the first cases in this Court construing the Fourteenth Amendment, decided shortly after its adoption, the Court interpreted it as proscribing all state-imposed discriminations against the Negro race. The doctrine of "separate but equal" did not make its appearance in this Court until 1896 in the case of *Plessy v. Ferguson*, supra [already cited above], involving not education but transportation. American courts have since labored with the doctrine for over half a century. In this Court, there have been six cases involving the "separate but equal" doctrine in the field of public education. In *Cumming v. County Board of Education* and *Gong Lum v. Rice* the validity of the doctrine itself was not challenged. In more recent cases, all on the graduate school level, inequality was found in that specific benefits enjoyed by white students were denied to Negro students of the same educational qualifications. In none of these cases was it necessary to re-examine the doctrine to grant relief to the Negro plaintiff. And in *Sweatt v. Painter* ... the Court expressly reserved decision on the question whether *Plessy v. Ferguson* should be held inapplicable to public education.

In the instant cases, that question is directly presented. Here, unlike *Sweatt v. Painter*, there are findings below that the Negro and white schools involved have been equalized, or are being equalized, with respect to buildings, curricula, qualifications and salaries of teachers, and other "tangible" factors. Our decision, therefore, cannot turn on merely a comparison of these tangible factors in the Negro and white schools involved in each of the cases. We must look instead to the effect of segregation itself on public education.

In approaching this problem, we cannot turn the clock back to 1868 when the Amendment was adopted, or even to 1896 when *Plessy v. Ferguson* was written. We must consider public education in the light of its full development and its present place in American life throughout the Nation. Only in this way can it be determined if segregation in public schools deprives these plaintiffs of the equal protection of the laws.

Education Must Be Equal

Today, education is perhaps the most important function of state and local governments. Compulsory school attendance laws and the great expenditures for education . . . demonstrate our recognition of the importance of education to our democratic society. It is required in the performance of our most basic public responsibilities, even service in the armed forces. It is the very foundation of good citizenship. Today it is a principal instrument in awakening the child to cultural values, in preparing him for later professional training, and in helping him to adjust normally to his environment. In these days, it is doubtful that any child may reasonably be expected to succeed in life if he is denied the opportunity of an education. Such an opportunity, where the state has undertaken to provide it, is a right which must be made available to all on equal terms.

We come then to the question presented: Does segregation of children in public schools solely on the basis of race, even though the physical facilities and other "tangible" factors may be equal, deprive the children of the minority group of equal educational opportunities? We believe that it does.

In *Sweatt v. Painter*, supra, in finding that a segregated law school for Negroes could not provide them equal educational opportunities, this Court relied in large part on "those qualities which are incapable of objective measurement but which make for greatness in a law school." In *McLaurin v. Oklahoma State Regents*, supra, the Court, in requiring that a Negro admitted to a white graduate school be treated like all other students, again resorted to intangible considerations: ". . . his ability to study, to engage in discussions and exchange views with other students, and, in general, to learn his profession." Such considerations apply with added force to children in grade and high schools. To separate them from others of similar age and qualifications solely because of their race generates a feeling of inferiority as to their status in the community that may affect their hearts and minds in a way unlikely ever to be undone. The effect of this separation on their educational opportunities was well stated by a finding in the Kansas case by a court which nevertheless felt compelled to rule against the Negro plaintiffs:

> Segregation of white and colored children in public schools has a detrimental effect upon the colored children. The impact is greater when it has the sanction of the law; for the policy of separating the races is usually interpreted as denoting the inferiority of the negro group. A sense of inferiority affects the motivation of a child to learn. Segregation with the sanction of law, therefore, has a tendency to [retard] the educational and mental development of negro children and to deprive them of some of the benefits they would receive in a racial[ly] integrated school system.

Whatever may have been the extent of psychological knowledge at the time of *Plessy v. Ferguson*, this finding is amply supported by modern authority. Any language in *Plessy v. Ferguson* contrary to this finding is rejected.

We conclude that in the field of public education the doctrine of "separate but equal" has no place. Separate educational facilities are inherently unequal. Therefore, we hold that the plaintiffs and others similarly situated for whom the actions have been brought are, by reason of the segregation complained of, deprived of the equal protection of the laws guaranteed by the Fourteenth Amendment. This disposition makes unnecessary any discussion whether such segregation also violates the Due Process Clause of the Fourteenth Amendment.

Because these are class actions, because of the wide applicability of this decision, and because of the great variety of local conditions, the formulation of decrees in these cases presents problems of considerable complexity. On reargument, the consideration of appropriate relief was necessarily subordinated to the primary question—the constitutionality of segregation in public education. We have now announced that such segregation is a denial of the equal protection of the laws. . . .

It is so ordered.

| "Brown *required the country to acknowledge and define race relations."*

A Participant in the *Brown* Case Assesses Its Legacy

Personal Narrative

Cheryl Brown Henderson

Cheryl Brown Henderson is one of three daughters of the late Oliver Brown, the named plaintiff in the landmark Brown v. Board of Education *case. In the following viewpoint she comments on the legacy of the Supreme Court's decision declaring that racially segregated schools are unconstitutional. She asserts the importance of educating future generations about the case, the significance of which goes beyond education reform. Henderson characterizes the* Brown *case as forcing the nation to address race relations as well as defining the intent of the Fourteenth Amendment.*

Our nation is fast approaching a watershed year. In Kansas, as well as all over the country, we will witness the 50th anniversary of the landmark U.S. Supreme Court decision in *Oliver L.*

Brown et al. v. the Board of Education of Topeka (KS) et al. on May 17, 2004.

We should pay particular attention to the *Brown* decision, because of the weight placed on its importance by legal scholars and historians alike. With *Brown,* the high court issued a definitive interpretation of the 14th amendment to our Constitution, making it clear that every individual in this country was entitled to "equal protection under the laws" without regard to race, ethnicity, gender, disability, age or any other circumstance. In addition, their decision had a profound impact on our society by making it illegal to practice racial segregation. *Brown* laid a foun-

Cheryl Brown Henderson (right) makes a speech before introducing President George W. Bush in Topeka, Kansas, on the fiftieth anniversary of the Brown v. Board of Education *ruling.* © Larry W. Smith/Getty Images.

dation for ending legal discrimination on any basis as evidenced by the legislation that followed a decade later beginning with the Civil Rights Act of 1964.

In order to prepare and educate our state and nation and bring a better understanding of the coming anniversary of *Brown,* we created a 50th Anniversary state coalition. This coalition will plan programs to focus our attention on *Brown*'s role in race relations, education and access to public accommodations. The goal is to have a better-informed citizenry with respect to this historic milestone.

In order to ensure a federal presence in the 50th anniversary of *Brown,* the Brown Foundation worked along with our Kansas Congressional delegation to pass legislation which established a *Brown v. Board of Education* 50th Anniversary Presidential Commission. President [George W.] Bush signed this bill on September 18, 2001. After appointments to this body were confirmed in August of 2002, the commission began its work. . . . The commission will plan commemorations and engage in programs for the purpose of educating the public about the significance of the *Brown* decision. . . .

The centerpiece of the 50th Anniversary commemoration will be the grand opening of the *Brown v. Board of Education* National Historic Site, a unit of the National Park Service. . . . The National Park [Service] will make certain that the *Brown* decision is interpreted for generations to come.

On a personal note, my family, much like the country, came to gradually understand the importance of the *Brown* decision. It became most evident with the passage of legislation like the Civil Rights Act of 1964, the Voting Rights Act of 1965 and Title IX in 1972, because each of these acts [is] based on the Court's edict of equal protection under the laws. My father was recruited by his childhood friend, who at the time was legal counsel for the Topeka [Kansas] NAACP, and joined 12 other parents as plaintiffs in this class action suit; we bear this legacy proudly. Being the family of the namesake of this judicial turning point comes with a responsibility to teach and never let the country forget what it took for some of its citizens to be afforded their constitutional rights.

Finally, I categorize the importance of *Brown* in this way; it represents three critical aspects in the pursuit of our democratic ideals. First education reform, because education is fundamental to citizenship. Second, *Brown* required the country to acknowledge and define race relations. Third, the Court ultimately directed the country in what course it had to follow with respect to the inclusive intent of the 14th Amendment to the Constitution. *Brown* asserted the rights of African American people to be full partners in social, political and communal structures.

The *Brown* decision and the civil rights movement in the United States inspired and galvanized human rights struggles around the world. Other countries often emulate what happens in the United States, the leader of the free world. The *Brown* federal commission hopes to catalogue the thousands of commemorative programs that will occur in communities, school districts, universities and organizations across the country.

The *Brown* decision was merely a catalyst—positive relations require more than one willing participant. For many of us, this is a once in a lifetime opportunity to have a national platform for conveying to the citizens and leaders of our country that at the heart of positive race relations is a sense of unity, respect and acceptance.

| "*The law is contrary to the mandate of the First, and in violation of the Fourteenth, amendment to the Constitution.*"

Prohibiting the Teaching of Evolution Is a Violation of the Establishment Clause

The Supreme Court's Decision

Abe Fortas

In 1928 the Arkansas legislature passed a law prohibiting teachers in public or other state-run schools from teaching human evolution. Decades later, Susan Epperson, an Arkansas public school teacher, sued, claiming the law violated her First Amendment right to free speech as well as the First Amendment's Establishment Clause, which states that the establishment of a state religion is unconstitutional. In 1968 the Supreme Court found that the 1928 law violated the Establishment Clause. The justices ruled that the law had been based solely on fundamentalist Christian beliefs, which argue that evolutionary theories contradict the biblical account of Creation. Abe Fortas served on the Supreme Court from 1965 to 1969.

Abe Fortas, Majority opinion, *Epperson v. Arkansas*, US Supreme Court, November 12, 1968. Copyright © 1968 The Supreme Court of the United States.

Appellant [Susan] Epperson, an Arkansas public school teacher, brought this action for declaratory and injunctive relief challenging the constitutionality of Arkansas' "anti-evolution" statute. That statute makes it unlawful for a teacher in any state-supported school or university to teach or to use a textbook that teaches "that mankind ascended or descended from a lower order of animals." The State Chancery Court held the statute [to be] an abridgment of free speech, violating the First and Fourteenth Amendments. The State Supreme Court, expressing no opinion as to whether the statute prohibits "explanation" of the theory or only teaching that the theory is true, reversed the Chancery Court. In a two-sentence opinion it sustained the statute as within the State's power to specify the public school curriculum. Held: The statute violates the Fourteenth Amendment, which embraces the First Amendment's prohibition of state laws respecting an establishment of religion.

(a)   The Court does not decide whether the statute is unconstitutionally vague, since, whether it is construed to prohibit explaining the Darwinian theory or teaching that it is true, the law conflicts with the Establishment Clause.

(b)   The sole reason for the Arkansas law is that a particular religious group considers the evolution theory to conflict with the account of the origin of man set forth in the Book of Genesis.

(c)   The First Amendment mandates governmental neutrality between religion and religion, and between religion and nonreligion.

(d)   A State's right to prescribe the public school curriculum does not include the right to prohibit teaching a scientific theory or doctrine for reasons that run counter to the principles of the First Amendment.

(e)   The Arkansas law is not a manifestation of religious neutrality. . . .

The Arkansas Supreme Court Ruling

This appeal challenges the constitutionality of the "anti-evolution" statute which the State of Arkansas adopted in 1928 to prohibit the teaching in its public schools and universities of the theory that man evolved from other species of life. The statute was a product of the upsurge of "fundamentalist" religious fervor of the twenties. The Arkansas statute was an adaptation of the famous Tennessee "monkey law" which that State adopted in 1925. The constitutionality of the Tennessee law was upheld by the Tennessee Supreme Court in the celebrated Scopes case in 1927.

The Arkansas law makes it unlawful for a teacher in any state-supported school or university "to teach the theory or doctrine that mankind ascended or descended from a lower order of animals," or "to adopt or use in any such institution a textbook that teaches" this theory. Violation is a misdemeanor and subjects the violator to dismissal from his position.

The present case concerns the teaching of biology in a high school in Little Rock [Arkansas]. According to the testimony, until the events here in litigation, the official textbook furnished for the high school biology course did not have a section on the Darwinian Theory. Then, for the academic year 1965–1966, the school administration, on recommendation of the teachers of biology in the school system, adopted and prescribed a textbook which contained a chapter setting forth "the theory about the origin . . . of man from a lower form of animal."

Susan Epperson, a young woman who graduated from Arkansas' school system and then obtained her master's degree in zoology at the University of Illinois, was employed by the Little Rock school system in the fall of 1964 to teach 10th-grade biology at Central High School. At the start of the next academic year, 1965, she was confronted by the new textbook (which one surmises from the record was not unwelcome to her). She faced at least a literal dilemma because she was supposed to use the new textbook for classroom instruction and presumably to teach the statutorily condemned chapter; but to do so would be a criminal offense and subject her to dismissal.

She instituted the present action in the Chancery Court of the State, seeking a declaration that the Arkansas statute is void and enjoining the State and the defendant officials of the Little Rock school system from dismissing her for violation of the statute's provisions. H.H. Blanchard, a parent of children attending the public schools, intervened in support of the action.

The Chancery Court, in an opinion by Chancellor Murray O. Reed, held that the statute violated the Fourteenth Amendment to the United States Constitution. The court noted that this Amendment encompasses the prohibitions upon state interference with freedom of speech and thought which are contained in the First Amendment. Accordingly, it held that the challenged statute is unconstitutional because, in violation of the First Amendment, it "tends to hinder the quest for knowledge, restrict the freedom to learn, and restrain the freedom to teach."

Biology teacher Susan Epperson challenged Arkansas's ban on teaching evolution in 1966. © AP Images.

In this perspective, the Act, it held, was an unconstitutional and void restraint upon the freedom of speech guaranteed by the Constitution.

On appeal, the Supreme Court of Arkansas reversed. . . . It sustained the statute as an exercise of the State's power to specify the curriculum in public schools. It did not address itself to the competing constitutional considerations.

Appeal was duly prosecuted to this Court under 28 U.S.C. 1257. Only Arkansas and Mississippi have such "anti-evolution" or "monkey" laws on their books. There is no record of any prosecutions in Arkansas under its statute. It is possible that the statute is presently more of a curiosity than a vital fact of life in these States. Nevertheless, the present case was brought, the appeal as of right is properly here, and it is our duty to decide the issues presented.

The Statute Cannot Stand

At the outset, it is urged upon us that the challenged statute is vague and uncertain and therefore within the condemnation of the Due Process Clause of the Fourteenth Amendment. The contention that the Act is vague and uncertain is supported by language in the brief opinion of Arkansas' Supreme Court. That court, perhaps reflecting the discomfort which the statute's quixotic prohibition necessarily engenders in the modern mind, stated that it "expresses no opinion" as to whether the Act prohibits "explanation" of the theory of evolution or merely forbids "teaching that the theory is true." Regardless of this uncertainty, the court held that the statute is constitutional.

On the other hand, counsel for the State, in oral argument in this Court, candidly stated that, despite the State Supreme Court's equivocation, Arkansas would interpret the statute "to mean that to make a student aware of the theory . . . just to teach that there was such a theory" would be grounds for dismissal and for prosecution under the statute; and he said "that the Supreme Court of Arkansas' opinion should be interpreted in that manner."

He said: "If Mrs. Epperson would tell her students that 'Here is Darwin's theory, [which states] that man ascended or descended from a lower form of being,' then I think she would be under this statute liable for prosecution."

In any event, we do not rest our decision upon the asserted vagueness of the statute. On either interpretation of its language, Arkansas' statute cannot stand. It is of no moment whether the law is deemed to prohibit mention of Darwin's theory, or to forbid any or all of the infinite varieties of communication embraced within the term "teaching." Under either interpretation, the law must be stricken because of its conflict with the constitutional prohibition of state laws respecting an establishment of religion or prohibiting the free exercise thereof. The overriding fact is that Arkansas' law selects from the body of knowledge a particular segment which it proscribes for the sole reason that it is deemed to conflict with a particular religious doctrine; that is, with a particular interpretation of the Book of Genesis by a particular religious group. . . .

An Unconstitutional Law

There is and can be no doubt that the First Amendment does not permit the State to require that teaching and learning must be tailored to the principles or prohibitions of any religious sect or dogma. In *Everson v. Board of Education*, this Court, in upholding a state law to provide free bus service to school children, including those attending parochial schools, said: "Neither [a State nor the Federal Government] can pass laws which aid one religion, aid all religions, or prefer one religion over another" (1947).

At the following Term of Court, in *McCollum v. Board of Education* (1948), the Court held that Illinois could not release pupils from class to attend classes of instruction in the school buildings in the religion of their choice. This, it said, would involve the State in using tax-supported property for religious purposes, thereby breaching the "wall of separation" which, according to Jefferson, the First Amendment was intended to erect

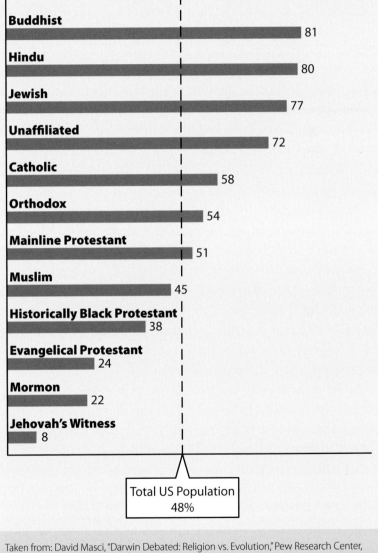

VIEWS ON EVOLUTION

This bar graph shows the percentage of those of various religious affiliations who agree that evolution is the best explanation for the origins of human life on earth.

Buddhist — 81
Hindu — 80
Jewish — 77
Unaffiliated — 72
Catholic — 58
Orthodox — 54
Mainline Protestant — 51
Muslim — 45
Historically Black Protestant — 38
Evangelical Protestant — 24
Mormon — 22
Jehovah's Witness — 8

Total US Population
48%

Taken from: David Masci, "Darwin Debated: Religion vs. Evolution," Pew Research Center, February 4, 2009. pewforum.org.

between church and state. While study of religions and of the Bible from a literary and historic viewpoint, presented objectively as part of a secular program of education, need not collide with the First Amendment's prohibition, the State may not adopt programs or practices in its public schools or colleges which "aid or oppose" any religion. This prohibition is absolute. It forbids alike the preference of a religious doctrine or the prohibition of theory which is deemed antagonistic to a particular dogma. As Mr. Justice [Tom] Clark stated in *Joseph Burstyn, Inc. v. Wilson*, "the state has no legitimate interest in protecting any or all religions from views distasteful to them . . ." (1952). The test was stated as follows in *Abington School District v. Schempp*: "[W]hat are the purpose and the primary effect of the enactment? If either is the advancement or inhibition of religion then the enactment exceeds the scope of legislative power as circumscribed by the Constitution."

These precedents inevitably determine the result in the present case. The State's undoubted right to prescribe the curriculum for its public schools does not carry with it the right to prohibit, on pain of criminal penalty, the teaching of a scientific theory or doctrine where that prohibition is based upon reasons that violate the First Amendment. It is much too late to argue that the State may impose upon the teachers in its schools any conditions that it chooses, however restrictive they may be of constitutional guarantees.

In the present case, there can be no doubt that Arkansas has sought to prevent its teachers from discussing the theory of evolution because it is contrary to the belief of some that the Book of Genesis must be the exclusive source of doctrine as to the origin of man. No suggestion has been made that Arkansas' law may be justified by considerations of state policy other than the religious views of some of its citizens. It is clear that fundamentalist sectarian conviction was and is the law's reason for existence. Its antecedent, Tennessee's "monkey law," candidly stated its purpose: to make it unlawful "to teach any theory that denies the story of the Divine Creation of man as taught in the Bible, and to teach instead that man has descended from a lower order of animals." Perhaps the sensational publicity attendant upon the Scopes trial induced Arkansas to adopt less explicit language. It eliminated Tennessee's reference to "the story of the Divine Creation of man" as taught in the Bible, but there is no doubt that the motivation for the law was the same: to suppress the teaching of a theory which, it was thought, "denied" the divine creation of man.

Arkansas' law cannot be defended as an act of religious neutrality. Arkansas did not seek to excise from the curricula of its schools and universities all discussion of the origin of man. The law's effort was confined to an attempt to blot out a particular theory because of its supposed conflict with the Biblical account, literally read. Plainly, the law is contrary to the mandate of the First, and in violation of the Fourteenth, Amendment to the Constitution.

The judgment of the Supreme Court of Arkansas is reversed.

> *"In this case, the purpose of the Creationism Act was to restructure the science curriculum to conform with a particular religious viewpoint."*

Teaching Creationism Is a Violation of the Constitution

The Supreme Court's Decision

William Brennan

During the 1980s, Louisiana passed a law that prohibited the teaching of the theory of evolution in public schools unless creation science was taught in conjunction. Although the law did not require the teaching of creation science or evolution, if either subject was taught, then the teacher was obligated to give instruction in the other as well. Using the Lemon *test, a three-point test established in* Lemon v. Kurtzman *(1971), the justices ruled in the 1987* Edwards v. Aguillard *decision that the law violated the Establishment Clause of the First Amendment, which lays the foundation for the separation of church and state principle. William Brennan served on the Supreme Court from 1956 to 1990.*

The Creationism Act forbids the teaching of the theory of evolution in public schools unless accompanied by instruction in "creation science." No school is required to teach evolution or creation science. If either is taught, however, the other must also be taught. The theories of evolution and creation science are statutorily defined as "the scientific evidences for [creation or evolution] and inferences from those scientific evidences."

Appellees, who include parents of children attending Louisiana public schools, Louisiana teachers, and religious leaders, challenged the constitutionality of the Act in District Court, seeking an injunction and declaratory relief. Appellants, Louisiana officials charged with implementing the Act, defended on the ground that the purpose of the Act is to protect a legitimate secular interest, namely, academic freedom. Appellees attacked the Act as facially invalid because it violated the Establishment Clause and made a motion for summary judgment. The District Court granted the motion. The court held that there can be no valid secular reason for prohibiting the teaching of evolution, a theory historically opposed by some religious denominations. The court further concluded that "the teaching of 'creation-science' and 'creationism,' as contemplated by the statute, involves teaching 'tailored to the principles' of a particular religious sect or group of sects." The District Court therefore held that the Creationism Act violated the Establishment Clause either because it prohibited the teaching of evolution or because it required the teaching of creation science with the purpose of advancing a particular religious doctrine.

The Court of Appeals affirmed. The court observed that the statute's avowed purpose of protecting academic freedom was inconsistent with requiring, upon risk of sanction, the teaching of creation science whenever evolution is taught. The court found that the Louisiana Legislature's actual intent was "to discredit evolution by counterbalancing its teaching at every turn with the teaching of creationism, a religious belief." Because the Creationism Act was thus a law furthering a particular religious belief, the Court of Appeals held that the Act violated the Establishment Clause. . . .

The *Lemon* Test

The Establishment Clause forbids the enactment of any law "respecting an establishment of religion." The Court has applied a three-pronged test to determine whether legislation comports with the Establishment Clause. First, the legislature must have adopted the law with a secular purpose. Second, the statute's principal or primary effect must be one that neither advances nor inhibits religion. Third, the statute must not result in an excessive entanglement of government with religion [*Lemon v. Kurtzman* (1971)]. State action violates the Establishment Clause if it fails to satisfy any of these prongs.

In this case, the Court must determine whether the Establishment Clause was violated in the special context of the public elementary and secondary school system. States and local school boards are generally afforded considerable discretion in operating public schools. "At the same time . . . we have necessarily recognized that the discretion of the States and local school boards in matters of education must be exercised in a manner that comports with the transcendent imperatives of the First Amendment" [*Board of Education, Island Trees Union Free School Dist. No. 26 v. Pico* (1982)].

The Court has been particularly vigilant in monitoring compliance with the Establishment Clause in elementary and secondary schools. Families entrust public schools with the education of their children, but condition their trust on the understanding that the classroom will not purposely be used to advance religious views that may conflict with the private beliefs of the student and his or her family. Students in such institutions are impressionable and their attendance is involuntary. The State exerts great authority and coercive power through mandatory attendance requirements, and because of the students' emulation of teachers as role models and the children's susceptibility to peer pressure. Furthermore, "[t]he public school is at once the symbol of our democracy and the most pervasive means for promoting our common destiny. In no activity of the State is it more vital to keep out divisive forces than in its schools . . ." [*Illinois ex rel. McCollum v. Board of Education* (1948)]. . . .

Therefore, in employing the three-pronged *Lemon* test, we must do so mindful of the particular concerns that arise in the context of public elementary and secondary schools. We now turn to the evaluation of the Act under the *Lemon* test.

The Purpose of the Act

Lemon's first prong focuses on the purpose that animated adoption of the Act. "The purpose prong of the *Lemon* test asks whether government's actual purpose is to endorse or disapprove of religion" [*Lynch v. Donnelly* (1984)]. A governmental intention to promote religion is clear when the State enacts a law to serve a religious purpose. This intention may be evidenced by promotion of religion in general (Establishment Clause protects individual freedom of conscience to "select any religious faith or none at all"), or by advancement of a particular religious belief. . . . If the law was enacted for the purpose of endorsing religion, "no consideration of the second or third criteria [of *Lemon*] is necessary" [*Wallace v. Jaffree*]. In this case, appellants have identified no clear secular purpose for the Louisiana Act.

True, the Act's stated purpose is to protect academic freedom. This phrase might, in common parlance, be understood as referring to enhancing the freedom of teachers to teach what they will. The Court of Appeals, however, correctly concluded that the Act was not designed to further that goal. We find no merit in the State's argument that the "legislature may not [have] use[d] the terms 'academic freedom' in the correct legal sense. They might have [had] in mind, instead, a basic concept of fairness; teaching all of the evidence." Even if "academic freedom" is read to mean "teaching all of the evidence" with respect to the origin of human beings, the Act does not further this purpose. The goal of providing a more comprehensive science curriculum is not furthered either by outlawing the teaching of evolution or by requiring the teaching of creation science.

Does Not Advance Academic Freedom

While the Court is normally deferential to a State's articulation of a secular purpose, it is required that the statement of such purpose be sincere and not a sham. . . .

It is clear from the legislative history that the purpose of the legislative sponsor, Senator Bill Keith, was to narrow the science curriculum. During the legislative hearings, Senator Keith stated: "My preference would be that neither [creationism nor evolution] be taught." Such a ban on teaching does not promote—indeed, it undermines—the provision of a comprehensive scientific education.

It is equally clear that requiring schools to teach creation science with evolution does not advance academic freedom. The Act does not grant teachers a flexibility that they did not already possess to supplant the present science curriculum with the presentation of theories, besides evolution, about the origin of life. Indeed, the Court of Appeals found that no law prohibited Louisiana public school teachers from teaching any scientific theory. As the president of the Louisiana Science Teachers Association testified, "[a]ny scientific concept that's based on established fact can be included in our curriculum already, and no legislation allowing this is necessary." The Act provides Louisiana schoolteachers with no new authority. Thus the stated purpose is not furthered by it.

The Alabama statute held unconstitutional in *Wallace v. Jaffree* is analogous. In *Wallace*, the State characterized its new law as one designed to provide a 1-minute period for meditation. We rejected that stated purpose as insufficient because a previously adopted Alabama law already provided for such a 1-minute period. Thus, in this case, as in *Wallace*, "[a]ppellants have not identified any secular purpose that was not fully served by [existing state law] before the enactment of [the statute in question]."

Furthermore, the goal of basic "fairness" is hardly furthered by the Act's discriminatory preference for the teaching of creation science and against the teaching of evolution. While requiring that curriculum guides be developed for creation science, the Act says nothing of comparable guides for evolution.

Similarly, resource services are supplied for creation science but not for evolution. Only "creation scientists" can serve on the panel that supplies the resource services. The Act forbids school boards to discriminate against anyone who "chooses to be a creation-scientist" or to teach "creationism," but fails to protect those who choose to teach evolution or any other noncreation science theory, or who refuse to teach creation science.

If the Louisiana Legislature's purpose was solely to maximize the comprehensiveness and effectiveness of science instruction, it would have encouraged the teaching of all scientific theories about the origins of humankind. But under the Act's requirements, teachers who were once free to teach any and all facets of this subject are now unable to do so. Moreover, the Act fails even to ensure that creation science will be taught, but instead requires the teaching of this theory only when the theory of evolution is taught. Thus we agree with the Court of Appeals' conclusion that the Act does not serve to protect academic freedom, but has the distinctly different purpose of discrediting "evolution by counterbalancing its teaching at every turn with the teaching of creationism. . . ."

Advancing a Religious Doctrine

We need not be blind in this case to the legislature's preeminent religious purpose in enacting this statute. There is a historic and contemporaneous link between the teachings of certain religious denominations and the teaching of evolution. It was this link that concerned the Court in *Epperson v. Arkansas* (1968), which also involved a facial challenge to a statute regulating the teaching of evolution. In that case, the Court reviewed an Arkansas statute that made it unlawful for an instructor to teach evolution or to use a textbook that referred to this scientific theory. Although the Arkansas antievolution law did not explicitly state

TEACHING EVOLUTION AND CREATIONISM

This table shows the hours devoted to human evolution, general evolution, and creationism or intelligent design in high school biology classes in 2007.

Hours	Human Evolution	General Evolutionary Processes	Creationism or Intelligent Design
Not covered at all	17%	2%	75%
1–2 hours	35%	9%	18%
3–5 hours	25%	25%	5%
6–10 hours	12%	26%	1%
11–15 hours	5%	18%	1%
16–20 hours	3%	11%	1%
21 hours or more	2%	9%	0%
Total	**100%**	**100%**	**100%**

Taken from: Michael B. Berkman, Julianna Sandell Pacheco, and Eric Plutzer, "Evolution and Creationism in America's Classrooms: A National Portrait," PLoS Biology, vol. 6, no. 5, May 2008, p. 922.

its predominate religious purpose, the Court could not ignore that "[t]he statute was a product of the upsurge of 'fundamentalist' religious fervor" that has long viewed this particular scientific theory as contradicting the literal interpretation of the Bible.

Dr. Maude Stout teaches creationism at Bob Jones University in Greenville, South Carolina. In 1987, the Supreme Court found that the Creationism Act was designed to narrow rather than broaden the educational curriculum. © Francis Miller/Time Life Pictures/Getty Images.

After reviewing the history of antievolution statutes, the Court determined that "there can be no doubt that the motivation for the [Arkansas] law was the same [as other antievolution statutes]: to suppress the teaching of a theory which, it was thought, 'denied' the divine creation of man." The Court found that there can be no legitimate state interest in protecting particular religions from scientific views "distasteful to them," and concluded "that the First Amendment does not permit the State to require that teaching and learning must be tailored to the principles or prohibitions of any religious sect or dogma."

These same historic and contemporaneous antagonisms between the teachings of certain religious denominations and the teaching of evolution are present in this case. The preeminent purpose of the Louisiana Legislature was clearly to advance the religious viewpoint that a supernatural being created humankind. The term "creation science" was defined as embracing this particular religious doctrine by those responsible for the passage of the Creationism Act. Senator Keith's leading expert on creation science, Edward Boudreaux, testified at the legislative hearings that the theory of creation science included belief in the existence of a supernatural creator. Senator Keith also cited testimony from other experts to support the creation-science view that "a creator [was] responsible for the universe and everything in it." The legislative history therefore reveals that the term "creation science," as contemplated by the legislature that adopted this Act, embodies the religious belief that a supernatural creator was responsible for the creation of humankind.

Furthermore, it is not happenstance that the legislature required the teaching of a theory that coincided with this religious view. The legislative history documents that the Act's primary purpose was to change the science curriculum of public schools in order to provide persuasive advantage to a particular religious doctrine that rejects the factual basis of evolution in its entirety. The sponsor of the Creationism Act, Senator Keith, explained during the legislative hearings that his disdain for the theory of evolution resulted from the support that evolution supplied to views contrary to his own religious beliefs. According to Senator Keith, the theory of evolution was consonant with the "cardinal principle[s] of religious humanism, secular humanism, theological liberalism, aetheistism [sic]." The state senator repeatedly stated that scientific evidence supporting his religious views should be included in the public school curriculum to redress the fact that the theory of evolution incidentally coincided with what he characterized as religious beliefs antithetical to his own. The legislation therefore sought to alter the science curriculum to reflect endorsement of a religious view that is antagonistic to the theory of evolution.

In this case, the purpose of the Creationism Act was to restructure the science curriculum to conform with a particular religious viewpoint. Out of many possible science subjects taught in the public schools, the legislature chose to affect the teaching of the one scientific theory that historically has been opposed by certain religious sects. As in *Epperson*, the legislature passed the Act to give preference to those religious groups which have as one of their tenets the creation of humankind by a divine creator. The "overriding fact" that confronted the Court in *Epperson* was "that Arkansas' law selects from the body of knowledge a particular segment which it proscribes for the sole reason that it is deemed to conflict with . . . a particular interpretation of the Book of Genesis by a particular religious group." Similarly, the Creationism Act is designed either to promote the theory of creation science, which embodies a particular religious tenet by requiring that creation science be taught whenever evolution is taught or to prohibit the teaching of a scientific theory disfavored by certain religious sects by forbidding the teaching of evolution when creation science is not also taught. The Establishment Clause, however, "forbids alike the preference of a religious doctrine or the prohibition of theory which is deemed antagonistic to a particular dogma." Because the primary purpose of the Creationism Act is to advance a particular religious belief, the Act endorses religion in violation of the First Amendment. . . .

The Louisiana Creationism Act advances a religious doctrine by requiring either the banishment of the theory of evolution from public school classrooms or the presentation of a religious viewpoint that rejects evolution in its entirety. The Act violates the Establishment Clause of the First Amendment because it seeks to employ the symbolic and financial support of government to achieve a religious purpose. The judgment of the Court of Appeals therefore is affirmed.

> *"It can hardly be argued that either students or teachers shed their constitutional rights to freedom of speech or expression at the schoolhouse gate."*

Students Have Rights While at School

The Supreme Court's Decision

Abe Fortas

In December 1965 three students, John F. Tinker, Mary Beth Tinker, and Christopher Eckhardt, formed a plan to wear black armbands to their schools in protest of the Vietnam War. After learning of this plan, the principals of their Des Moines, Iowa, schools banned armbands in their schools. All three students wore the armbands in spite of the ban and were suspended from school. The students challenged the suspensions in court, and after they lost their case in the US District Court and the Court of Appeals, the US Supreme Court heard their arguments in 1968. The Supreme Court decided that the school policy amounted to a violation of the First Amendment right to free speech. The Tinker *Test is still used to determine whether students' First Amendment rights have been violated. Abe Fortas served on the Supreme Court from 1965 to 1969.*

Abe Fortas, Majority opinion, *Tinker v. Des Moines Independent Community School District*, US Supreme Court, February 24, 1969. Copyright © 1969 The Supreme Court of the United States.

Petitioner John F. Tinker, 15 years old, and petitioner Christopher Eckhardt, 16 years old, attended high schools in Des Moines, Iowa. Petitioner Mary Beth Tinker, John's sister, was a 13-year-old student in junior high school.

In December 1965, a group of adults and students in Des Moines held a meeting at the Eckhardt home. The group determined to publicize their objections to the hostilities in Vietnam and their support for a truce by wearing black armbands during the holiday season and by fasting on December 16 and New Year's Eve. Petitioners and their parents had previously engaged in similar activities, and they decided to participate in the program.

The principals of the Des Moines schools became aware of the plan to wear armbands. On December 14, 1965, they met and adopted a policy that any student wearing an armband to school would be asked to remove it, and if he refused he would be suspended until he returned without the armband. Petitioners were aware of the regulation that the school authorities adopted.

On December 16, Mary Beth and Christopher wore black armbands to their schools. John Tinker wore his armband the next day. They were all sent home and suspended from school until they would come back without their armbands. They did not return to school until after the planned period for wearing armbands had expired—that is, until after New Year's Day.

This complaint was filed in the United States District Court by petitioners, through their fathers, under [section] 1983 of Title 42 of the United States Code. It prayed for [requested] an injunction restraining the respondent school officials and the respondent members of the board of directors of the school district from disciplining the petitioners, and it sought nominal damages. After an evidentiary hearing the District Court dismissed the complaint. It upheld the constitutionality of the school authorities' action on the ground that it was reasonable in order to prevent disturbance of school discipline. The court referred to but expressly declined to follow the Fifth Circuit's holding in a similar case that the wearing of symbols like the armbands cannot be prohibited unless it "materially and substantially interfere[s] with the requirements of appropriate discipline in the operation of the school" [*Burnside v. Byars* (1966)].

On appeal, the Court of Appeals for the Eighth Circuit considered the case en banc [with all judges present]. The court was equally divided, and the District Court's decision was accordingly affirmed, without opinion. We granted certiorari [an order by a higher court in response to an appellant's request for review of a ruling by a lower court or other judicial body].

Student and Teacher Rights Are Upheld

The District Court recognized that the wearing of an armband for the purpose of expressing certain views is the type of symbolic act that is within the Free Speech Clause of the First Amendment. As we shall discuss, the wearing of armbands in the circumstances of this case was entirely divorced from actually or potentially disruptive conduct by those participating in it. It was closely akin to "pure speech" which, we have repeatedly held, is entitled to comprehensive protection under the First Amendment.

First Amendment rights, applied in light of the special characteristics of the school environment, are available to teachers and students. It can hardly be argued that either students or teachers shed their constitutional rights to freedom of speech or expression at the schoolhouse gate. This has been the unmistakable holding of this Court for almost 50 years. In *Meyer v. Nebraska* (1923), and *Bartels v. Iowa* (1923), this Court, in opinions by Mr. Justice [James Clark] McReynolds, held that the Due Process Clause of the Fourteenth Amendment prevents States from forbidding the teaching of a foreign language to young students. Statutes to this effect, the Court held, unconstitutionally interfere with the liberty of teacher, student, and parent.

In *West Virginia v. Barnette* ... this Court held that under the First Amendment, the student in public school may not be compelled to salute the flag. Speaking through Mr. Justice [Robert H.] Jackson, the Court said:

> The Fourteenth Amendment, as now applied to the States, protects the citizen against the State itself and all of its creatures— Boards of Education not excepted. These have, of course, important, delicate, and highly discretionary functions, but none that they may not perform within the limits of the Bill of Rights. That they are educating the young for citizenship is reason for scrupulous protection of Constitutional freedoms of the individual, if we are not to strangle the free mind at its source and teach youth to discount important principles of our government as mere platitudes.

On the other hand, the Court has repeatedly emphasized the need for affirming the comprehensive authority of the States and of school officials, consistent with fundamental constitutional safeguards, to prescribe and control conduct in the schools. Our problem lies in the area where students in the exercise of First Amendment rights collide with the rules of the school authorities.

No Disruption of Learning

The problem posed by the present case does not relate to regulation of the length of skirts or the type of clothing, to hair style, or deportment. It does not concern aggressive, disruptive action or even group demonstrations. Our problem involves direct, primary First Amendment rights akin to "pure speech."

The school officials banned and sought to punish petitioners for a silent, passive expression of opinion, unaccompanied by any disorder or disturbance on the part of petitioners. There is here no evidence whatever of petitioners' interference, actual or nascent, with the schools' work or of collision with the rights of other students to be secure and to be let alone. Accordingly, this case does not concern speech or action that intrudes upon the work of the schools or the rights of other students.

The *Tinker* Standard

Doctrinally, *Tinker*'s standard focuses on a single, dispositive issue: student expression may not be suppressed unless school officials reasonably conclude that the speech "would materially and substantially disrupt the work and discipline of the school." Two factors have been crucial to the lower courts applying *Tinker.* First, can the school district point to past incidents arising out of similar speech that establish a "well-founded expectation of disruption"? Second, if a school cannot pinpoint past incidents, can it demonstrate substantial facts that reasonably support a "specific and significant fear of disruption"? If a school can establish "past incidents" or a "specific and significant fear of disruption," the *Tinker* standard is satisfied, and a policy restricting student expression is constitutional.

Geoffrey A. Starks, "Tinker's Tenure in the
School Setting: The Case for Applying O'Brien
to Content-Neutral Regulations," Yale Law
Journal, *August 30, 2010.*

Only a few of the 18,000 students in the school system wore the black armbands. Only five students were suspended for wearing them. There is no indication that the work of the schools or any class was disrupted. Outside the classrooms, a few students made hostile remarks to the children wearing armbands, but there were no threats or acts of violence on school premises.

The District Court concluded that the action of the school authorities was reasonable because it was based upon their fear of a disturbance from the wearing of the armbands. But, in our system, undifferentiated fear or apprehension of disturbance is not enough to overcome the right to freedom of expression. Any departure from absolute regimentation may cause trouble. Any variation from the majority's opinion may inspire fear. Any word spoken, in class, in the lunchroom, or on the campus, that deviates from the views of another person may start an argument or cause a disturbance. But our Constitution says we must take this risk; and our history says that it is this sort of hazardous freedom—this kind of openness—that is the basis of our national strength and of the independence and vigor of Americans who grow up and live in this relatively permissive, often disputatious, society.

In order for the State in the person of school officials to justify prohibition of a particular expression of opinion, it must be able to show that its action was caused by something more than a mere desire to avoid the discomfort and unpleasantness that always accompany an unpopular viewpoint. Certainly where there is no finding and no showing that engaging in the forbidden conduct would "materially and substantially interfere with the requirements of appropriate discipline in the operation of the school," the prohibition cannot be sustained [*Burnside v. Byars*].

In the present case, the District Court made no such finding, and our independent examination of the record fails to yield evidence that the school authorities had reason to anticipate that the wearing of the armbands would substantially interfere with the work of the school or impinge upon the rights of other students. Even an official memorandum prepared after the suspension that listed the reasons for the ban on wearing the armbands made no reference to the anticipation of such disruption.

On the contrary, the action of the school authorities appears to have been based upon an urgent wish to avoid the controversy which might result from the expression, even by the silent symbol of armbands, of opposition to this Nation's part in the conflagration in Vietnam. It is revealing, in this respect, that the meeting at which the school principals decided to issue the contested regulation was called in response to a student's statement to the journalism teacher in one of the schools that he wanted to write an article on Vietnam and have it published in the school paper. (The student was dissuaded.)

Prohibiting the Expression of a Particular Opinion Is Not Permissible

It is also relevant that the school authorities did not purport to prohibit the wearing of all symbols of political or controversial significance. The record shows that students in some of the schools wore buttons relating to national political campaigns, and some even wore the Iron Cross, traditionally a symbol of Nazism. The order prohibiting the wearing of armbands did not extend to these. Instead, a particular symbol—black armbands worn to exhibit opposition to this Nation's involvement in Vietnam—was singled out for prohibition. Clearly, the prohibition of expression of one particular opinion, at least without evidence that it is necessary to avoid material and substantial interference with schoolwork or discipline, is not constitutionally permissible.

In our system, state-operated schools [are not allowed to] be enclaves of totalitarianism. School officials do not possess absolute authority over their students. Students in school as well as out of school are "persons" under our Constitution. They are possessed of fundamental rights which the State must respect, just as they themselves must respect their obligations to the State. In our system, students may not be regarded as closed-circuit recipients of only that which the State chooses to communicate. They may not be confined to the expression of those sentiments that are officially approved. In the absence of a specific showing of constitutionally valid reasons to regulate their speech, students are entitled to freedom of expression of their views. As Judge [Walter] Gewin, speaking for the Fifth Circuit, said, school officials cannot suppress "expressions of feelings with which they do not wish to contend" [*Burnside v. Byars*]. . . .

The principle of these cases is not confined to the supervised and ordained discussion which takes place in the classroom. The principal use to which the schools are dedicated is to accommodate students during prescribed hours for the purpose of certain types of activities. Among those activities is personal intercommunication among the students. This is not only an inevitable part of the process of attending school; it is also an important part of the educational process. A student's rights, therefore, do not embrace merely the classroom hours. When he is in the cafeteria, or on the playing field, or on the campus during the authorized hours, he may express his opinions, even on controversial subjects like the conflict in Vietnam, if he does so without "materially and substantially interfer[ing] with the requirements of appropriate discipline in the operation of the school" and without colliding with the rights of others [*Burnside v. Byars*]. But conduct by the student, in class or out of it, which for any reason—whether it stems from time, place, or type of behavior— materially disrupts classwork or involves substantial disorder or invasion of the rights of others is, of course, not immunized by the constitutional guarantee of freedom of speech.

Under our Constitution, free speech is not a right that is given only to be so circumscribed that it exists in principle but not in fact. Freedom of expression would not truly exist if the right

Protesters burn draft cards during the Vietnam War. The petitioners in the Tinker *case wanted to protest at a time when such protests against the war were very common outside of school.* © Dick Swanson/Time Life Pictures/Getty Images.

could be exercised only in an area that a benevolent government has provided as a safe haven for crackpots. The Constitution says that Congress (and the States) may not abridge the right to free speech. This provision means what it says. We properly read it to permit reasonable regulation of speech-connected activities in carefully restricted circumstances. But we do not confine the permissible exercise of First Amendment rights to a telephone booth or the four corners of a pamphlet, or to supervised and ordained discussion in a school classroom.

If a regulation were adopted by school officials forbidding discussion of the Vietnam conflict, or the expression by any student of opposition to it anywhere on school property except as part of a prescribed classroom exercise, it would be obvious that the regulation would violate the constitutional rights of students, at least if it could not be justified by a showing that the students' activities would materially and substantially disrupt the work and discipline of the school. In the circumstances of the present case, the prohibition of the silent, passive "witness of the armbands," as one of the children called it, is no less offensive to the Constitution's guarantees.

As we have discussed, the record does not demonstrate any facts which might reasonably have led school authorities to forecast substantial disruption of or material interference with school activities, and no disturbances or disorders on the school premises in fact occurred. These petitioners merely went about their ordained rounds in school. Their deviation consisted only in wearing on their sleeve a band of black cloth, not more than two inches wide. They wore it to exhibit their disapproval of the Vietnam hostilities and their advocacy of a truce, to make their views known, and, by their example, to influence others to adopt them. They neither interrupted school activities nor sought to intrude in the school affairs or the lives of others. They caused discussion outside of the classrooms, but no interference with work and no disorder. In the circumstances, our Constitution does not permit officials of the State to deny their form of expression.

We express no opinion as to the form of relief which should be granted, this being a matter for the lower courts to determine. We reverse and remand for further proceedings consistent with this opinion.

Reversed and remanded.

> "I urge students to celebrate their right to speak out by becoming engaged in issues that are important to their lives, and to exercise their First Amendment rights."

A *Tinker* Participant Argues That Students' First Amendment Rights Remain in Jeopardy

Personal Narrative

Mary Beth Tinker, interviewed by Stephen J. Wermiel

In the following viewpoint Stephen J. Wermiel, co-chair of the Human Rights *editorial board, interviews Mary Beth Tinker. Tinker was one of the plaintiffs in* Tinker v. Des Moines Independent Community School District, *a case in which students fought for the right of freedom of expression in public schools. She argues that while the ruling in the case was significant at the time, students have lost their rights to freedom of expression in many ways in the decades that have followed. She urges students to speak up for their rights and expresses hope for the future.*

Human Rights: What's the state of student free speech or student rights more broadly as we approach the fortieth anniversary of Tinker?

Mary Beth Tinker: They are in about the same state as students' well-being overall, whether you're talking about health issues or educational quality or housing or access to clean air and water, which are not very good right now. And I'm speaking as a nurse who has worked primarily with young people.

For one thing, No Child Left Behind [a 2001 education reform law] has not been helpful in teaching students about their rights or helping them to model democratic behavior. Curricula directed toward standardized tests in math and science may "train" young people in certain skills, particularly test-taking skills, but are lacking in other areas. So, despite the valiant efforts of history and government teachers across the country, it is no wonder that we are seeing woefully poor indicators of students' knowledge of the First Amendment, for example.

Some states see rising test scores as success, but many of us who work with youths are skeptical. Critical thinking and creativity, which are so important to participatory democracy, have been sacrificed.

Forty Years of Change

How do you feel about the Tinker *case itself after forty years?*

The *Tinker* ruling said that students had the right to free speech and other First Amendment rights unless their speech was "substantially disruptive" or intruded on the rights of others. So that was a foundation, because it's not a very high standard.

Since then, school districts have claimed that various activities are disruptive or intrude on the rights of others. The ruling leaves a lot of leeway for principals and school boards to attempt to censor students, and they often succeed.

Regardless, of course, I am happy that the [Supreme Court under the leadership of Chief Justice Earl Warren] ruled in favor of students' rights. In a democracy, the people who are affected by decisions are supposed to be the ones who have the right to speak on their own behalf, and this should include young people. Today, I see so many examples of young people standing up for their own interests.

For example, students in Ohio recently developed the Ohio Youth Agenda, a collaboration of youths across the state [who are] advocating for improvement in schools, counseling, and education funding. Students in Maryland were featured in the *Washington Post* recently, picketing against a new polluting freeway near their school. Another Maryland girl, Sarah Boltuck, succeeded in getting state legislation passed that will allow seventeen-year-olds to register to vote if they will turn eighteen by the time of the election. Twenty thousand youths are affected.

At a school in Florida, students had to fight for the right to wear rainbow clothing and bring stickers to school. They eventually won. Alondra Jones, in California, challenged unfair funding of her school and changed the school funding system for the whole state. And these are just a few examples that come to mind.

Over the forty years, though, other cases have eroded the protection that Tinker *established. How do you feel about that?*

Free speech rights of students have been curtailed, certainly, but the erosion is not limited to students. And besides Court rulings like *Hazelwood, Morse v. Frederick*, or the recent *Jacobs* ruling in Nevada, students' free speech rights have been curtailed in other ways. For example, I understand that about 40 percent of high school newspapers have been eliminated in the last ten to fifteen years.

In the fortieth anniversary year of Tinker *next year [2009], what are you celebrating?*

I will be celebrating the spirit of young people and their creative energy in standing up for their rights against all odds, and their humor and concern, which are so needed in this current period. And I will be celebrating a Supreme Court that stood with young people to affirm their rights.

And what should students of the country think about or celebrate?

I urge students to celebrate their right to speak out by becoming engaged in issues that are important to their lives, and to exercise their First Amendment rights and, indeed, all their rights.

You've spent a lot of time speaking to student groups and accepting the mantle of a spokesperson for student rights since the Tinker *decision. How do you see that role?*

My parents put their beliefs into action, and they were examples to me. My father was a Methodist minister, and my parents later became Quakers. They spent their lives working for peace and justice. Over the years, I also met others and heard their stories about standing up for what they believed in. These people motivated and inspired me. So that is how I see my role with young people, to educate and inspire them. Besides teaching them basic civics, I tell them real stories about people, mostly young people, from the past and present, who have changed the world.

For example, I may tell them about Barbara Johns, who was sixteen in 1951 when she called an assembly at her school in Virginia, rallying students for better conditions at their school. She later became a plaintiff in the *Brown* case. Or I tell them about the children's march of 1904, where child factory workers presented Teddy Roosevelt with a demand to end their sweatshop conditions. These are just examples of the many true stories that I choose from.

And then I tell them about young people today who are in-volved in various issues, like the ones I talked about earlier, and others.

Hope for the Future

Are you hopeful that young people will continue to stand up for their rights, that the courts and the country will become more ap-preciative of the rights of students again?

Yes. I see examples all over the country of students who are stand-ing up for what they believe in, whether it's for peace, clean air, clean water, uniform policies, religious freedom, animal rights, gay rights, Darfur [a conflict involving accusations of mass rape and genocide by Sudan's government forces against non-Arab Sudanese]. There are so many issues students care about.

I hear about students who, themselves, wear different, mean-ingful symbols—whether it's T-shirts, armbands, or buttons. Some are involved in the political process, working for different candidates that support young people's issues. All of that's very heartening to me.

How about the role of lawyers, courts, and law in defending student rights? What do you think has happened over the last decades?

Young people cannot make progress without the support and al-liance of adults, whether they're lawyers or nurses, like myself, or parents or community partners. And so young people need to have supporters in the community who advocate for them also and who help them to advocate for themselves. That's the way I see the role of lawyers.

Adults can use their skills and talents to promote young people and teenagers, who need these skills more than ever in today's world. Because the condition of young people today is not good. There are so many indicators, whether health indicators or indicators of educational success—for example, graduation rates, college rates. I just heard statistics that around 50 percent of Washington, D.C., high school students are graduating. I understand that only around 9 percent of those high school students are completing a four-year college degree program.

Economic opportunities for young people are not good, and so many children go without health insurance. The Children's Health Insurance Program has been under attack. So many areas exist where young people really need advocates, especially legal advocates, and people with all kinds of skills and talents.

One of the great messages of Tinker *was not to fear protest—that school officials should accept protest as an essential part of democracy and even of education. Have we lost sight of that message?*

Well, I think the political climate in the country discourages young people from speaking up. Protest is only one of those ways that students might want to speak up. And I think it's a big mistake in a democracy to discourage people from being involved in the democratic process, in whatever form that may take.

Throughout history a lot of our progress has been the result of people who were considered dissidents in their time; without encouraging a climate where free speech and dissidents' voices flourish, we won't benefit as much as we could as a society. And we'll be held back in our own development and in relationship to other societies that are encouraging these kinds of expressions.

And what's your feeling about the Supreme Court's most recent decision—the Bong Hits case?

That case, where Joseph Frederick unfurled a banner saying "Bong Hits 4 Jesus," was about more than just the so-called frivolous message. When I spoke to him on the telephone before the case was argued at the Supreme Court, he told me how he came to put that on his banner. He said he did that because he had been studying the First Amendment and the Bill of Rights in school, and he wanted to test and see if he really had First Amendment rights or if it was just something that he had learned in school books.

So he wanted to put something on his banner, and if he had just said "Hooray for the Olympic torch," which was going by, he wouldn't have been able to test his rights. So he sure did pick something that would get the attention of the school and others: "Bong Hits 4 Jesus." But his real message was that students should have First Amendment rights. And that is a serious message.

I'm sorry to see that the Court has once again limited the rights of students, not only in terms of the content of the message, but also the school's jurisdiction seems to have been extended because Joseph was standing across the street from the school and there was some question about whether it was actually a school-sponsored event. That's a big issue being debated now in our country—how far does the school's jurisdiction reach? And this ruling seems to have extended that.

> *"If personalized instruction is being provided . . . the child is receiving a 'free appropriate publication education' as defined by the Act."*

Public Schools Need Only Provide Adequate Educational Opportunities for Students with Disabilities

The Supreme Court's Decision

William Rehnquist

Hendrick Hudson Board of Education v. Rowley *was the first Supreme Court case to take on the Education for All Handicapped Children Act (now known as the Individuals with Disabilities Education Act, or IDEA). Amy Rowley, a deaf student, is at the center of the case. Her parents argued that in addition to other accommodations, she should be provided an interpreter, at the school's expense, for all of her academic classes. The school denied their request, and eventually the Rowleys' case was heard by New York's federal district court. That court, as well as the US Court of Appeals, sided with the Rowleys. The Supreme Court, however, reversed the judgment. In the following majority opinion, Justice*

William Rehnquist, Majority opinion, *Hendrick Hudson Board of Education v. Rowley*, US Supreme Court, June 28, 1982. Copyright © 1982 The Supreme Court of the United States.

William Rehnquist asserts that providing an interpreter for every class goes beyond what should be expected of any school system, given that Amy was progressing well without one. The Court found that the Hendrick Hudson Central School District was in compliance with the law in providing all students "a free appropriate public education." William Rehnquist served on the Supreme Court from 1972 to 2005, serving as Chief Justice beginning in 1986.

This case arose in connection with the education of Amy Rowley, a deaf student at the Furnace Woods School in the Hendrick Hudson Central School District, Peekskill, N.Y. Amy has minimal residual hearing and is an excellent lip-reader. During the year before she began attending Furnace Woods, a meeting between her parents and school administrators resulted in a decision to place her in a regular kindergarten class in order to determine what supplemental services would be necessary to her education. Several members of the school administration prepared for Amy's arrival by attending a course in sign-language interpretation, and a teletype machine was installed in the principal's office to facilitate communication with her parents who are also deaf. At the end of the trial period it was determined that Amy should remain in the kindergarten class, but that she should be provided with an FM hearing aid which would amplify words spoken into a wireless receiver by the teacher or fellow students during certain classroom activities. Amy successfully completed her kindergarten year.

As required by the Act, an IEP [Individualized Education Program] was prepared for Amy during the fall of her first-grade year. The IEP provided that Amy should be educated in a regular classroom at Furnace Woods, should continue to use the FM hearing aid, and should receive instruction from a tutor for the deaf for one hour each day and from a speech therapist for three hours each week. The Rowleys agreed with parts of the IEP but insisted that Amy also be provided a qualified sign-language interpreter in all her academic classes in lieu of the assistance proposed in other parts of the IEP. Such an interpreter had been placed in Amy's kindergarten class for a 2-week experimental period, but the interpreter had reported that Amy did not need his services at that time. The school administrators likewise concluded that Amy did not need such an interpreter in her first-grade classroom. They reached this conclusion after consulting the school district's Committee on the Handicapped, which had received expert evidence from Amy's parents on the importance of a sign-language interpreter, received testimony from Amy's teacher and other persons familiar with her academic and social progress, and visited a class for the deaf.

The Findings of the Lower Courts

When their request for an interpreter was denied, the Rowleys demanded and received a hearing before an independent examiner. After receiving evidence from both sides, the examiner agreed with the administrators' determination that an interpreter was not necessary because "Amy was achieving educationally, academically, and socially" without such assistance. The examiner's decision was affirmed on appeal by the New York Commissioner of Education on the basis of substantial evidence in the record. Pursuant to the Act's provision for judicial review, the Rowleys then brought an action in the United States District Court for the Southern District of New York, claiming that the administrators' denial of the sign-language interpreter constituted a denial of the "free appropriate public education" guaranteed by the Act.

The District Court found that Amy "is a remarkably well-adjusted child" who interacts and communicates well with her classmates and has "developed an extraordinary rapport" with her teachers. It also found that "she performs better than the average child in her class and is advancing easily from grade to grade," but "that she understands considerably less of what goes on in class than she could if she were not deaf" and thus "is not learning as much, or performing as well academically, as she would without her handicap." This disparity between Amy's achievement and her potential led the court to decide that she was not receiving a "free appropriate public education," which the court defined as "an opportunity to achieve [her] full potential commensurate with the opportunity provided to other children." According to the District Court, such a standard "requires that the potential of the handicapped child be measured and compared to his or her performance, and that the resulting differential or 'shortfall' be compared to the shortfall experienced by nonhandicapped children." The District Court's definition arose from its assumption that the responsibility for "giv[ing] content to the requirement of an 'appropriate education'" had "been left entirely to the [federal] courts and the hearing officers."

A divided panel of the United States Court of Appeals for the Second Circuit affirmed. The Court of Appeals "agree[d] with the [D]istrict [C]ourt's conclusions of law," and held that its "findings of fact [were] not clearly erroneous."

We granted certiorari [a motion] to review the lower courts' interpretation of the Act. Such review requires us to consider two questions: What is meant by the Act's requirement of a "free appropriate public education"? And what is the role of state and federal courts in exercising the review granted by 20 U.S.C. 1415 [The Act]? . . .

"Free Appropriate Public Education"

According to the definitions contained in the Act, a "free appropriate public education" consists of educational instruction specially designed to meet the unique needs of the handicapped child, supported by such services as are necessary to permit the child "to benefit" from the instruction. Almost as a checklist for adequacy under the Act, the definition also requires that such instruction and services be provided at public expense and under public supervision, meet the State's educational standards, approximate the grade levels used in the State's regular education, and comport with the child's IEP. Thus, if personalized instruction is being provided with sufficient supportive services to

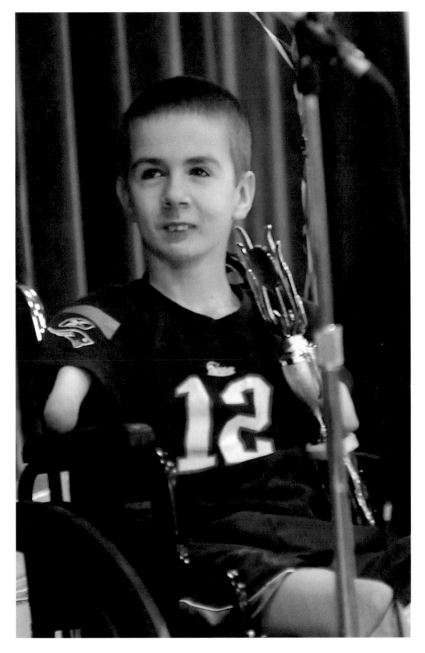

Nicholas Maxim receives an award for excellent penmanship despite having been born without lower arms. The Supreme Court ruled that public schools must provide adequate educational opportunity for students with disabilities, but not beyond the schools' capabilities. © AP Images/The Kennebec Journal, Andy Molloy.

permit the child to benefit from the instruction, and the other items on the definitional checklist are satisfied, the child is receiving a "free appropriate public education" as defined by the Act.

Other portions of the statute also shed light upon congressional intent. Congress found that of the roughly eight million handicapped children in the United States at the time of enactment, one million were "excluded entirely from the public school system" and more than half were receiving an inappropriate education. In addition, as mentioned . . . the Act requires States to extend educational services first to those children who are receiving no education and second to those children who are receiving an "inadequate education." When these express statutory findings and priorities are read together with the Act's extensive procedural requirements and its definition of "free appropriate public education," the face of the statute evinces a congressional intent to bring previously excluded handicapped children into the public education systems of the States and to require the States to adopt procedures which would result in individualized consideration of and instruction for each child.

Noticeably absent from the language of the statute is any substantive standard prescribing the level of education to be accorded handicapped children. Certainly the language of the statute contains no requirement like the one imposed by the lower courts—that States maximize the potential of handicapped children "commensurate with the opportunity provided to other children." That standard was expounded by the District Court without reference to the statutory definitions or even to the legislative history of the Act. . . .

Courts Should Not Impose Educational Methods on the States

A court's inquiry in suits brought under 1415(e)(2) [the Act] is twofold. First, has the State complied with the procedures set forth in the Act? And second, is the individualized educational program developed through the Act's procedures reasonably calculated to enable the child to receive educational benefits? If these requirements are met, the State has complied with the obligations imposed by Congress, and the courts can require no more.

In assuring that the requirements of the Act have been met, courts must be careful to avoid imposing their view of preferable educational methods upon the States. The primary responsibility for formulating the education to be accorded a handicapped child, and for choosing the educational method most suitable to the child's needs, was left by the Act to state and local educational agencies in cooperation with the parents or guardian of the child. The Act expressly charges States with the responsibility of "acquiring and disseminating to teachers and administrators of programs for handicapped children significant information derived from educational research, demonstration, and similar projects, and [of] adopting, where appropriate, promising educational practices and materials." In the face of such a clear statutory directive, it seems highly unlikely that Congress intended courts to overturn a State's choice of appropriate educational theories in a proceeding conducted pursuant to 1415(e)(2).

We previously have cautioned that courts lack the "specialized knowledge and experience" necessary to resolve "persistent and difficult questions of educational policy" [*San Antonio Independent School Dist. v. Rodriguez*]. We think that Congress shared that view when it passed the Act. As already demonstrated, Congress' intention was not that the Act displace the primacy of States in the field of education, but that States receive funds to assist them in extending their educational systems to the handicapped. Therefore, once a court determines that the requirements of the Act have been met, questions of methodology are for resolution by the States.

Students Are Protected

Entrusting a child's education to state and local agencies does not leave the child without protection. Congress sought to protect

TOTAL STUDENT POPULATION RECEIVING SPECIAL EDUCATION SERVICES, BY DISABILITY CATEGORY

This chart reflects an *Education Week* analysis of data from the US Department of Education, Office of Special Programs, Data Analysis System, 2002–2003.

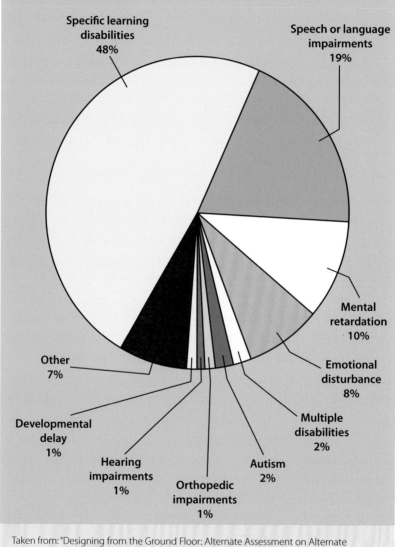

Specific learning disabilities
48%

Speech or language impairments
19%

Mental retardation
10%

Emotional disturbance
8%

Multiple disabilities
2%

Autism
2%

Orthopedic impairments
1%

Hearing impairments
1%

Developmental delay
1%

Other
7%

Taken from: "Designing from the Ground Floor: Alternate Assessment on Alternate Achievement Standards?" US Office of Special Education Programs. www.osepideasthatwork.org.

individual children by providing for parental involvement in the development of state plans and policies, and in the formulation of the child's individual educational program. As the Senate Report states:

> The Committee recognizes that in many instances the process of providing special education and related services to handicapped children is not guaranteed to produce any particular outcome. By changing the language [of the provision relating to individualized educational programs] to emphasize the process of parent and child involvement and to provide a written record of reasonable expectations, the Committee intends to clarify that such individualized planning conferences are a way to provide parent involvement and protection to assure that appropriate services are provided to a handicapped child. . . .

Applying these principles to the facts of this case, we conclude that the Court of Appeals erred in affirming the decision of the District Court. Neither the District Court nor the Court of Appeals found that petitioners had failed to comply with the procedures of the Act, and the findings of neither court would support a conclusion that Amy's educational program failed to comply with the substantive requirements of the Act. On the contrary, the District Court found that the "evidence firmly establishes that Amy is receiving an 'adequate' education, since she performs better than the average child in her class and is advancing easily from grade to grade." In light of this finding, and of the fact that Amy was receiving personalized instruction and related services calculated by the Furnace Woods school administrators to meet her educational needs, the lower courts should not have concluded that the Act requires the provision of a sign-language interpreter. Accordingly, the decision of the Court of Appeals is reversed, and the case is remanded for further proceedings consistent with this opinion.

So ordered.

"*Twenty five years later I know there
has been progress, but it is not
always evident.*"

The *Rowley* Plaintiff Recalls Her Family's Struggle with Her Public School

Personal Narrative

Amy June Rowley

*In the following viewpoint Amy June Rowley argues that while some
progress has been made for the education of disabled students in
the more than twenty-five years since her case was decided by the
Supreme Court, not nearly enough has been done. Rowley's parents went to court to seek greater accommodation for their daughter, who is deaf, from the Hendrick Hudson Board of Education in
New York. While lower courts supported the Rowleys, the Supreme
Court sided with the school board, asserting that Amy's school had
done enough under the law to give her an adequate education.
Rowley discusses her memories of those events and her attitudes
towards accommodations for deaf students today.*

Shortly after my parents learned I was deaf, the Education for All Handicapped Children Act, also known as Public Law 94-142, was passed in 1975. This legislation opened the door for disabled children to receive a free and appropriate public education in the least restrictive environment. My parents looked at this new development as an opportunity for me to be mainstreamed and receive an education like that delivered to hearing students. My mom certainly thought this was a better option than the deaf school because, after she learned I was deaf and began to educate me at home, I progressed normally, like hearing children with hearing parents. . . .

Making Accommodations

When I started kindergarten, my parents expected that an interpreter would be present in my class. When one was not there, my parents asked why one had not been provided. These inquiries created tension between the school district and my parents. My parents only wanted what they thought was best for me, a sign language interpreter to help me fully understand my teacher's spoken words. Hendrick Hudson School District was advised by its lawyer to exhaust all other options first. My mother was not willing to put my education on hold while everyone could agree on exactly what I needed. She talked with my teachers every day and made sure at home that I learned what was taught at school. Thus, in every sense of the word, I was home schooled even though I was also attending Furnace Woods School.

Eventually an agreement was reached that placed an interpreter in the classroom on a "trial basis" for four weeks.

> One day this man shows up in my class. I know he is the interpreter because my mom has told me he will be coming. But I am scared. I don't know what an interpreter is. I have never seen one before. I am only five, and I don't know what I am supposed to do with him. He also looks scary. He is very tall to anyone who is little like me, and he is wearing standard

interpreter attire of all black clothes. But I don't know that white interpreters wear dark colors to contrast with their skin color. No one in kindergarten is wearing all black so there must be something wrong with him. I am even more scared. I am only so eager to walk away and keep myself occupied with other doings. Once in a while I quickly steal a glance at him and see him signing. I wonder why. I did not understand that he was signing what the teacher was saying.

To further complicate things, there were several observers in class, and I knew somehow that they were there because of the man in black. I could not wait until the entourage and the oddly dressed, tall man would leave so my kindergarten class could get back to normal. Due to my reaction, the interpreter was removed from my classroom after only two weeks. The tension between my parents and the school district was heating up. . . .

The controversial IEP [individualized education plan] included providing speech classes to improve my ability to make others understand me, but this did not help *me* understand *others*. Wasn't that the point? I was required to wear an FM system with the teacher wearing a microphone. The FM system certainly amplified everything, but I heard only sounds. I could understand nothing. Simple amplification of the sounds did not allow comprehension of the meaning of the sounds. I think it is sometimes difficult for hearing people to understand that hearing aids and FM systems do not have the same effect as eyeglasses. I imagine the noises I heard every day sounded like loud power tools to hearing people. This constantly bugged me, and I was happy to turn the noises off. I recall many times that the noises in my head certainly were a distraction as I watched the teacher. I remember reading that the school contended that I had a lot of residual hearing so they felt it was their obligation to make sure I was able to use it. That comment was a light bulb moment for me. It showed me how much hearing people really don't understand what deaf people actually hear. Every deaf person has a different audiogram [an audiogram charts the intensity of sound that a person can detect at various frequencies], and every deaf person reacts differently to their environment. If two deaf people with a similar audiogram were compared based on their audiograms only, one would find a lot of similarities. However, if one looks at both people to see how they function and how they communicate, the audiogram is often not an accurate representation of who deaf people are. . . .

An Interpreter Makes a Big Difference

With second grade out of the way, I was on to a new start in third grade. The overall environment improved for me because the school and my parents seemed to have stopped fighting. There were fewer disruptions to my class, and we settled into everyday routines easily. In the lawsuit, the school district lost at the district court level and again at the Court of Appeals. After they lost the appeal, the school district was required to provide me with an interpreter. Having an interpreter in class could have been considered a "new distraction," but the interpreter quickly inserted herself into our everyday routine. Soon many of my classmates and I could not imagine our class without her. For the first time, I really enjoyed school. I was able to follow along perfectly in classroom discussions, and my interpreter made sure to interpret everything, including my classmates' conversations.

My interpreter, Fran Miller, had deaf parents so she grew up communicating in sign language. Not only was she fluent in signing, she was also a skilled interpreter and fully understood how to be a language mediator. She did just that, mediating exchanges among the other students, the teacher and me. I felt friendships blossoming, and I could communicate and follow group conversations. Because I was fluent in sign language, the interpreter opened up a new avenue of complete accessibility for me. I enjoyed school now. I looked forward to recess. The interpreter would follow me out and help me and other children figure out what we wanted to do. Before Fran Miller became my interpreter I had always followed the other children outside. They usually wanted to play kickball, but I was often not included. I would go to the playground and play alone or with a few other children. Now, when other children were in a group discussing what they wanted to do, I could be a part of the group. My interpreter also interpreted those conversations. I finally felt I had a voice because I could say I wanted to play kickball, and they would make sure I was involved. An added bonus of having an interpreter in the classroom meant that, when I got home from school, I only had to do my homework. I no longer had to work with my mother when I got home to relearn everything I was supposed to have learned in class that day. Now I really had a lot more time to play and "just be a kid." Third grade was a really good year.

School seemed really good, and life "seemed back to normal," but things were actively brewing in the background. . . .

The Supreme Court Battle and the Aftermath

In March 1982, while I was still in fourth grade, the United States Supreme Court heard the oral argument in the case between Hendrick Hudson School District and my parents. My parents' lawyer, Michael Chatoff, was the first deaf person ever to argue before the Supreme Court. Michael became deaf during law school due to tumors on his auditory nerves. Surgery to remove the tumors cut his auditory nerves, and he became permanently deaf. He struggled with neurofibromatosis, but it did not keep him from becoming a lawyer. Through chance, he met my parents and decided to take on our case. He never charged my parents any legal fees, which would have been huge by the time the case finally came to an end. Since he became deaf as an adult, he preferred to talk instead of signing. English was his first language. The Supreme Court arranged for the court proceedings to be transferred to a computer by a transcriptionist so Michael could read everything that was going on in real time. This was the first time such a venture had been undertaken. It is now common practice in courts all over America.

During the summer between fourth grade and fifth grade, the Supreme Court announced that the two previous decisions of the lower courts in my parents' favor were overturned. The Supreme Court sided with the school district, finding that the school did provide me with adequate services to make sure I was passing from grade to grade. For the Court, a free and appropriate public education did not mean I was entitled to reach my full potential as the gifted child that I was. It just meant that as long as I was passing, I was doing fine.

My parents had already decided to move to New Jersey. There was no reason to stay in Peekskill, New York. I would never have an interpreter in school there. My father commuted between New York and New Jersey every day for many years, so it seemed logical to move closer to where my father worked. In New Jersey, there was a day school for the deaf where many deaf children were mainstreamed. However, before we could move, I had to stick out one more year at Furnace Woods. . . .

When my parents put their house up for sale, the school district found out that we were moving and put a lien on our house to recover their costs in the litigation. We moved anyway, but my parents were not able to sell their house. The lien did not make matters easier. The conflict between the school district and my parents continued and became a dog-fight. Living in New York was bad for my family, and it was quickly getting worse.

The move to New Jersey was the best thing that happened to my family. I started attending school with other deaf kids. For the first time I truly didn't feel alone. I had an interpreter in all my classes. My brother had many friends who didn't care that his parents and his sister were deaf. They saw deaf students every day so the idea of deaf families was not such a foreign concept for them. Finally, I was no longer abnormal just because I was deaf.

I remember more than I would like to remember about my experience at Furnace Woods. I believe that I am supposed to remember so I can share my story in the hope that other children do not have to experience the same things I did. My experience informs the kind of decisions I make today as an adult. If a conflict arises and I know that I will have to put someone in an uncomfortable situation, I am more likely to avoid it. However, conflict and discomfort can't always be avoided. I wish both sides had not had to go into litigation. I wish that we had not had to move to find a new school district so that my needs could be met.

Children should be allowed to be children. Too often children are robbed of their right to grow up without the weight of the world on their shoulders. I know the weight of my world was squashing me in elementary school as my family and I pursued the educational experience I needed and deserved. Many times I wanted to play or be like the little kid I should have been, but I was expected to be just the opposite. With the case going all the way to the Supreme Court, I got a lot of national attention from the media. I didn't ask for that. People ask me if this was all worth it. Would I do this again? I was faced with that decision with my own children who are deaf. The school district I first worked with informed me that they wanted my oldest daughter to be able to function without an interpreter by the time she entered school. In my mind I was thinking that the school wanted to make her hearing. They wanted to deprive me and her of communication. I had to explain to the school that American Sign Language is not a detriment to my daughter's education but actually an advantage that helps her thrive in school. Twenty five years ago my parents asked for an interpreter for the exact same reasons. Twenty five years later I know there has been progress, but it is not always evident. So would I do it again? Not at the expense of my children.

> *"It is thus difficult to conceive of a rational justification for penalizing these children for their presence within the United States."*

All Children Have a Right to an Education, Regardless of Their Immigration Status

The Supreme Court's Decision

William Brennan

In 1975 Texas passed a law denying a free public education to the children of illegal immigrants and gave school districts the right to forbid those students access to classrooms. Seven years later the Supreme Court decided against the state of Texas, arguing that children of illegal immigrants should not be punished for actions their parents have taken. Furthermore, the five-to-four majority of justices asserted that by prohibiting these children an education, Texas was preventing them from learning about US culture and gaining future life opportunities. William Brennan served on the Supreme Court from 1956 to 1990.

William Brennan, Majority opinion, *Plyler v. Doe,* US Supreme Court, June 15, 1982. Copyright © 1982 The Supreme Court of the United States.

The question presented by these cases is whether, consistent with the Equal Protection Clause of the Fourteenth Amendment, Texas may deny to undocumented school-age children the free public education that it provides to children who are citizens of the United States or legally admitted aliens.

Since the late 19th century, the United States has restricted immigration into this country. Unsanctioned entry into the United States is a crime, and those who have entered unlawfully are subject to deportation. But despite the existence of these legal restrictions, a substantial number of persons have succeeded in unlawfully entering the United States, and now live within various States, including the State of Texas.

In May 1975, the Texas Legislature revised its education laws to withhold from local school districts any state funds for the education of children who were not "legally admitted" into the United States. The 1975 revision also authorized local school districts to deny enrollment in their public schools to children not "legally admitted" to the country. These cases involve constitutional challenges to those provisions.

Plyler v. Doe

This is a class action, filed in the United States District Court for the Eastern District of Texas in September 1977, on behalf of certain school-age children of Mexican origin residing in Smith County, [Texas], who could not establish that they had been legally admitted into the United States. The action complained of the exclusion of plaintiff children from the public schools of the Tyler Independent School District. The Superintendent and members of the Board of Trustees of the School District were named as defendants; the State of Texas intervened as a party-defendant. After certifying a class consisting of all undocumented school-age children of Mexican origin residing within the School District, the District Court preliminarily enjoined defendants from denying a free education to members of the plaintiff class. In December 1977, the court conducted an extensive hearing on plaintiffs' motion for permanent injunctive relief.

In considering this motion, the District Court made extensive findings of fact. The court found that neither 21.031 [the 1975 Texas law] nor the School District policy implementing it had "either the purpose or effect of keeping illegal aliens out of the State of Texas." Respecting defendants' further claim that 21.031 was simply a financial measure designed to avoid a drain on the State's fisc [treasury], the court recognized that the increases in population resulting from the immigration of Mexican nationals into the United States had created problems for the public schools of the State, and that these problems were exacerbated by the special educational needs of immigrant Mexican children. The court noted, however, that the increase in school enrollment was primarily attributable to the admission of children who were legal residents. It also found that while the "exclusion of all undocumented children from the public schools in Texas would eventually result in economies [savings] at some level," funding from both the State and Federal governments was based primarily on the number of children enrolled. In net effect then, barring undocumented children from the schools would save money, but it would "not necessarily" improve "the quality of education." The court further observed that the impact of 21.031 was borne primarily by a very small subclass of illegal aliens, "entire families who have migrated illegally and—for all practical purposes— permanently to the United States." Finally, the court noted that under current laws and practices "the illegal alien of today may well be the legal alien of tomorrow," and that without an education, these undocumented children, "[a]lready disadvantaged as a result of poverty, lack of English-speaking ability, and undeniable racial prejudices . . . will become permanently locked into the lowest socio-economic class."

Image on next pages: Undocumented immigrant teenagers in Douglasville, Georgia, protest against 2011 laws that crack down on illegal immigration. © AP Images/David Goldman.

The District Court held that illegal aliens were entitled to the protection of the Equal Protection Clause of the Fourteenth Amendment, and that 21.031 violated that Clause. Suggesting that "the state's exclusion of undocumented children from its public schools . . . may well be the type of invidiously motivated state action for which the suspect classification doctrine was designed," the court held that it was unnecessary to decide whether the statute would survive a "strict scrutiny" analysis because, in any event, the discrimination embodied in the statute was not supported by a rational basis. The District Court also concluded that the Texas statute violated the Supremacy Clause.

The Court of Appeals for the Fifth Circuit upheld the District Court's injunction. The Court of Appeals held that the District Court had erred in finding the Texas statute pre-empted by federal law. With respect to equal protection, however, the Court of Appeals affirmed in all essential respects the analysis of the District Court, concluding that 21.031 was "constitutionally infirm regardless of whether it was tested using the mere rational basis standard or some more stringent test." We noted probable jurisdiction. . . .

Children Should Not Be Punished

Sheer incapability or lax enforcement of the laws barring entry into this country, coupled with the failure to establish an effective bar to the employment of undocumented aliens, has resulted in the creation of a substantial "shadow population" of illegal migrants—numbering in the millions—within our borders. This situation raises the specter of a permanent caste of undocumented resident aliens, encouraged by some to remain here as a source of cheap labor, but nevertheless denied the benefits that our society makes available to citizens and lawful residents. The existence of such an underclass presents most difficult problems for a Nation that prides itself on adherence to principles of equality under law.

The children who are plaintiffs in these cases are special members of this underclass. Persuasive arguments support the

ESTIMATES OF THE NUMBER OF CHILDREN IN THE UNITED STATES, BY PARENTS' STATUS, 2009	Number (millions)	Percent
All children (17 and younger)	74.5	100%
US-born parents	57.5	77%
Immigrant parents	17.1	23%
Legal immigrant parents	11.9	16%
Unauthorized immigrant parents	5.1	7%

A child has unauthorized immigrant parents if either parent is unauthorized; a child has US-born parents if all identified parents are US born. Numbers may not total due to rounding.

Taken from: "Unauthorized Immigrants and Their U.S.-Born Children," Pew Hispanic Center, August 11, 2010, p. 1.

view that a State may withhold its beneficence from those whose very presence within the United States is the product of their own unlawful conduct. These arguments do not apply with the same force to classifications imposing disabilities on the minor children of such illegal entrants. At the least, those who elect to enter our territory by stealth and in violation of our law should be prepared to bear the consequences, including, but not limited to, deportation. But the children of those illegal entrants are not comparably situated. Their "parents have the ability to conform their conduct to societal norms," and presumably the ability to remove themselves from the State's jurisdiction; but the children who are plaintiffs in these cases "can affect neither their parents' conduct nor their own status" [*Trimble v. Gordon* (1977)]. Even if the State found it expedient to control the conduct of adults by acting against their children, legislation directing the onus of a parent's misconduct against his children does not comport with fundamental conceptions of justice. . . .

Of course, undocumented status is not irrelevant to any proper legislative goal. Nor is undocumented status an absolutely immutable characteristic since it is the product of conscious, indeed unlawful, action. But 21.031 is directed against children and imposes its discriminatory burden on the basis of a legal characteristic over which children can have little control. It is thus difficult to conceive of a rational justification for penalizing these children for their presence within the United States. Yet that appears to be precisely the effect of 21.031.

Public education is not a "right" granted to individuals by the Constitution. But neither is it merely some governmental "benefit" indistinguishable from other forms of social welfare legislation. Both the importance of education in maintaining our basic institutions, and the lasting impact of its deprivation on the life of the child, mark the distinction. The "American people have always regarded education and [the] acquisition of knowledge as matters of supreme importance" [*Meyer v. Nebraska* (1923)]. We have recognized "the public schools as a most vital civic institution for the preservation of a democratic system of government" [*Abington School District v. Schempp* (1963)], and as the primary vehicle for transmitting "the values on which our society rests" [*Ambach v. Norwick* (1979)]. "[A]s . . . pointed out early in our history . . . some degree of education is necessary to prepare citizens to participate effectively and intelligently in our open political system if we are to preserve freedom and independence" [*Wisconsin v. Yoder* (1972)]. And these historic "perceptions of the public schools as inculcating fundamental values necessary to the maintenance of a democratic political system have been confirmed by the observations of social scientists "[*Ambach v. Norwick*]. In addition, education provides the basic tools by which individuals might lead economically productive lives to the benefit of us all. In sum, education has a fundamental role in maintaining the fabric of our society. We cannot ignore the significant social costs borne by our Nation when select groups are denied the means to absorb the values and skills upon which our social order rests. . . .

If the State is to deny a discrete group of innocent children the free public education that it offers to other children residing within its borders, that denial must be justified by a showing that it furthers some substantial state interest. No such showing was made here. Accordingly, the judgment of the Court of Appeals in each of these cases is affirmed.

> "*Educators are entitled to exercise greater control over this second form of student expression [that includes school-sponsored publications].*"

School Administrators Have the Right to Edit the Content of Student Publications

The Supreme Court's Decision

Byron White

Hazelwood East High School in Missouri was at the center of a 1980s debate about student speech and journalism rights. Spectrum, *the student-run, school-sponsored newspaper, was edited by Cathy Kuhlmeier, a student. When pages of the May 13, 1983, issue were presented to the school principal, Robert E. Reynolds, he ordered that two articles slated to appear in that edition not be published based on what he considered objectionable content. Kuhlmeier and two former students took the case to court. The district court ruled against the students, deciding that their First Amendment rights had not been violated. Subsequently, the court of appeals reversed that decision, agreeing with the students. Ultimately, the Supreme Court decided that the principal's actions did not constitute a violation of the students' First Amendment rights to free speech be-*

Byron White, Majority opinion, *Hazelwood School District et al. v. Kuhlmeier et al.*, US Supreme Court, January 13, 1988. Copyright © 1988 The Supreme Court of the United States.

cause Reynolds acted on legitimate concerns over the privacy of those discussed in the articles and about the inappropriate nature of one of the articles. Byron White served on the Supreme Court from 1962 to 1993.

This case concerns the extent to which educators may exercise editorial control over the contents of a high school newspaper produced as part of the school's journalism curriculum.

Background

Petitioners are the Hazelwood School District in St. Louis County, Missouri; various school officials; Robert Eugene Reynolds, the principal of Hazelwood East High School; and Howard Emerson, a teacher in the school district. Respondents are three former Hazelwood East students who were staff members of *Spectrum*, the school newspaper. They contend that school officials violated their First Amendment rights by deleting two pages of articles from the May 13, 1983, issue of *Spectrum*.

Spectrum was written and edited by the Journalism II class at Hazelwood East. The newspaper was published every three weeks or so during the 1982–1983 school year. More than 4,500 copies of the newspaper were distributed during that year to students, school personnel, and members of the community.

The Board of Education allocated funds from its annual budget for the printing of *Spectrum*. These funds were supplemented by proceeds from sales of the newspaper. The printing expenses during the 1982–1983 school year totaled $4,668.50; revenue from sales was $1,166.84. The other costs associated with the newspaper—such as supplies, textbooks, and a portion of the journalism teacher's salary—were borne entirely by the Board.

The Journalism II course was taught by Robert Stergos for most of the 1982–1983 academic year. Stergos left Hazelwood East to take a job in private industry on April 29, 1983, when the May 13 [1983] edition of *Spectrum* was nearing completion, and petitioner Emerson took his place as newspaper adviser for the remaining weeks of the term.

The practice at Hazelwood East during the spring 1983 semester was for the journalism teacher to submit page proofs of each *Spectrum* issue to Principal Reynolds for his review prior to publication. On May 10 [1983], Emerson delivered the proofs of the May 13 edition to Reynolds, who objected to two of the articles scheduled to appear in that edition. One of the stories described three Hazelwood East students' experiences with pregnancy; the other discussed the impact of divorce on students at the school.

Reynolds was concerned that, although the pregnancy story used false names "to keep the identity of these girls a secret," the pregnant students still might be identifiable from the text. He also believed that the article's references to sexual activity and birth control were inappropriate for some of the younger students at the school. In addition, Reynolds was concerned that a student identified by name in the divorce story had complained that her father "wasn't spending enough time with my mom, my sister and I" prior to the divorce, "was always out of town on business or out late playing cards with the guys," and "always argued about everything" with her mother. Reynolds believed that the student's parents should have been given an opportunity to respond to these remarks, or to consent to their publication. He was unaware that Emerson had deleted the student's name from the final version of the article.

Reynolds believed that there was no time to make the necessary changes in the stories before the scheduled press run, and that the newspaper would not appear before the end of the school year if printing were delayed to any significant extent. He concluded that his only options under the circumstances were to publish a four-page newspaper instead of the planned six-page newspaper, eliminating the two pages on which the offending stories appeared, or to publish no newspaper at all. Accordingly, he directed Emerson to withhold from publication the two pages containing the stories on pregnancy and divorce. He informed his superiors of the decision, and they concurred.

Respondents subsequently commenced this action in the United States District Court for the Eastern District of Missouri, seeking a declaration that their First Amendment rights had been violated, injunctive relief, and monetary damages. After a bench trial, the district court denied an injunction, holding that no First Amendment violation had occurred. . . .

The court found that Principal Reynolds' concern that the pregnant students' anonymity would be lost and their privacy invaded was "legitimate and reasonable," given "the small number of pregnant students at Hazelwood East and several identifying characteristics that were disclosed in the article." The court held that Reynolds' action was also justified "to avoid the impression that [the school] endorses the sexual norms of the subjects" and to shield younger students from exposure to unsuitable material. The deletion of the article on divorce was seen by the court as a reasonable response to the invasion of privacy concerns raised by the named student's remarks. Because the article did not indicate that the student's parents had been offered an opportunity to respond to her allegations, said the court, there was cause for "serious doubt that the article complied with the rules of fairness which are standard in the field of journalism and which were covered in the textbook used in the Journalism II class." Furthermore, the court concluded that Reynolds was justified in deleting two full pages of the newspaper, instead of deleting only the pregnancy and divorce stories or requiring that those stories be modified to address his concerns, based on his "reasonable belief that he had to make an immediate decision and that there was no time to make modifications to the articles in question."

The Court of Appeals for the Eighth Circuit reversed. The court held at the outset that *Spectrum* was not only "a part of the school adopted curriculum," but also a public forum, because the newspaper was "intended to be and operated as a conduit for student viewpoint." The court then concluded that *Spectrum*'s status as a public forum precluded school officials from censoring its contents except when "'necessary to avoid material and substantial interference with school work or discipline . . . or the rights of others.'"

The Court of Appeals found "no evidence in the record that the principal could have reasonably forecast that the censored articles or any materials in the censored articles would have materially disrupted classwork or given rise to substantial disorder in the school."

School officials were entitled to censor the articles on the ground that they invaded the rights of others, according to the court, only if publication of the articles could have resulted in tort liability [that is, a lawsuit against] to the school. The court concluded that no tort action for libel or invasion of privacy could have been maintained against the school by the subjects of the two articles or by their families. Accordingly, the court held that school officials had violated respondents' First Amendment rights by deleting the two pages of the newspaper.

We granted certiorari [review], and we now reverse.

Rights of Students in School Are Not the Same as Those of Adults

[As stated in *Tinker v. Des Moines*] Students in the public schools do not "shed their constitutional rights to freedom of speech or expression at the schoolhouse gate." They cannot be punished merely for expressing their personal views on the school premises—whether "in the cafeteria, or on the playing field, or on the campus during the authorized hours"—unless school authorities have reason to believe that such expression will "substantially interfere with the work of the school or impinge upon the rights of other students."

We have nonetheless recognized that the First Amendment rights of students in the public schools "are not automatically coextensive with the rights of adults in other settings," [in] *Bethel School District No. 403 v. Fraser*, and must be "applied in light of

The Supreme Court ruled in Hazelwood *that administrators may censor school newspapers if the content may cause a disruption in the school's educational process.* © AP Images/ Alan Diaz.

the special characteristics of the school environment" [*Tinker*]. A school need not tolerate student speech that is inconsistent with its "basic educational mission" [*Fraser*], even though the government could not censor similar speech outside the school. Accordingly, we held in *Fraser* that a student could be disciplined for having delivered a speech that was "sexually explicit" but not legally obscene at an official school assembly, because the school was entitled to "disassociate itself" from the speech in a manner that would demonstrate to others that such vulgarity is "wholly inconsistent with the 'fundamental values' of public school education." We thus recognized that "[t]he determination of what manner of speech in the classroom or in school assembly is inappropriate properly rests with the school board," rather than with the federal courts. It is in this context that respondents' First Amendment claims must be considered.

Public Forum or Student Project?

We deal first with the question whether *Spectrum* may appropriately be characterized as a forum for public expression. The public schools do not possess all of the attributes of streets, parks, and other traditional public forums that "time out of mind, have been used for purposes of assembly, communicating thoughts between citizens, and discussing public questions" [*Hague v. CIO* (1939)]. Hence, school facilities may be deemed to be public forums only if school authorities have "by policy or by practice" opened those facilities "for indiscriminate use by the general public" [*Perry Education Assn. v. Perry Local Educators' Assn.* (1983)], or by some segment of the public, such as student organizations. If the facilities have instead been reserved for other intended purposes, "communicative or otherwise," then no public forum has been created, and school officials may impose reasonable restrictions on the speech of students, teachers, and other members of the school community. . . .

School officials did not deviate in practice from their policy that production of *Spectrum* was to be part of the educational curriculum, and a "regular classroom Activit[y]." The District Court found that Robert Stergos, the journalism teacher during most of the 1982–1983 school year, "both had the authority to exercise, and in fact exercised, a great deal of control over *Spectrum*." For example, Stergos selected the editors of the newspaper, scheduled publication dates, decided the number of pages for each issue, assigned story ideas to class members, advised students on the development of their stories, reviewed the use of quotations, edited stories, selected and edited the letters to the editor, and dealt with the printing company. Many of these decisions were made without consultation with the Journalism II students. . . .

Moreover, after each *Spectrum* issue had been finally approved by Stergos or his successor, the issue still had to be reviewed by Principal Reynolds prior to publication. Respondents' assertion that they had believed that they could publish "practically anything" in *Spectrum* was therefore dismissed by the District Court as simply "not credible." These factual findings are amply supported by the record, and were not rejected as clearly erroneous by the Court of Appeals . . . .

Authority over School-Sponsored Publications

The question whether the First Amendment requires a school to tolerate particular student speech—the question that we addressed in *Tinker*—is different from the question whether the First Amendment requires a school affirmatively to promote particular student speech. The former question addresses educators' ability to silence a student's personal expression that happens to occur on the school premises. The latter question concerns educators' authority over school-sponsored publications, theatrical productions, and other expressive activities that students, parents, and members of the public might reasonably perceive to bear the imprimatur of the school. These activities may fairly be characterized as part of the school curriculum, whether or not they occur in a traditional classroom setting, so long as they are supervised by faculty members and designed to impart particular knowledge or skills to student participants and audiences.

Educators are entitled to exercise greater control over this second form of student expression to assure that participants learn whatever lessons the activity is designed to teach, that readers or listeners are not exposed to material that may be inappropriate for their level of maturity, and that the views of the individual speaker are not erroneously attributed to the school. Hence, a school may, in its capacity as publisher of a school newspaper or producer of a school play, "disassociate itself" [*Fraser*], not only from speech that would "substantially interfere with [its] work . . . or impinge upon the rights of other students" [*Tinker*], but also from speech that is, for example, ungrammatical, poorly written, inadequately researched, biased or prejudiced, vulgar or profane, or unsuitable for immature audiences. A school must be able to set high standards for the student speech that is disseminated under its auspices—standards that may be higher than those demanded by some newspaper publishers or theatrical producers in the "real" world—and may refuse to disseminate student speech that does not meet those standards. In addition, a school must be able to take into account the emotional maturity of the intended audience in determining whether to disseminate student speech on potentially sensitive topics, which might range from the existence of Santa Claus in an elementary school setting to the particulars of teenage sexual activity in a high school setting. A school must also retain the authority to refuse to sponsor student speech that might reasonably be perceived to advocate drug or alcohol use, irresponsible sex, or conduct otherwise inconsistent with "the shared values of a civilized social order" [*Fraser*], or to associate the school with any position other than neutrality on matters of political controversy. . . .

Reynolds Acted Reasonably

We . . . conclude that Principal Reynolds acted reasonably in requiring the deletion from the May 13 [1983] issue of *Spectrum* of the pregnancy article, the divorce article, and the remaining articles that were to appear on the same pages of the newspaper.

The initial paragraph of the pregnancy article declared that "[a]ll names have been changed to keep the identity of these girls a secret." The principal concluded that the students' anonymity was not adequately protected, however, given the other identifying information in the article and the small number of pregnant students at the school. Indeed, a teacher at the school credibly testified that she could positively identify at least one of the girls, and possibly all three. It is likely that many students at Hazelwood East would have been at least as successful in identifying the girls. Reynolds therefore could reasonably have feared that the article violated whatever pledge of anonymity had been given to the pregnant students. In addition, he could reasonably have been concerned that the article was not sufficiently sensitive to the privacy interests of the students' boyfriends and parents, who were discussed in the article but who were given no opportunity to consent to its publication or to offer a response. The article did not contain graphic accounts of sexual activity. The girls did comment in the article, however, concerning their sexual histories and their use or nonuse of birth control. It was not unreasonable for the principal to have concluded that such frank talk was inappropriate in a school-sponsored publication distributed to 14-year-old freshmen and presumably taken home to be read by students' even younger brothers and sisters.

The student who was quoted by name in the version of the divorce article seen by Principal Reynolds made comments sharply critical of her father. The principal could reasonably have concluded that an individual publicly identified as an inattentive parent—indeed, as one who chose "playing cards with the guys" over home and family—was entitled to an opportunity to defend himself as a matter of journalistic fairness. These concerns were shared by both of *Spectrum*'s faculty advisers for the 1982–1983 school year, who testified that they would not have allowed the article to be printed without deletion of the student's name. . . .

In sum, we cannot reject as unreasonable Principal Reynolds' conclusion that neither the pregnancy article nor the divorce article was suitable for publication in *Spectrum*. Reynolds could reasonably have concluded that the students who had written and edited these articles had not sufficiently mastered those portions of the Journalism II curriculum that pertained to the treatment of controversial issues and personal attacks, the need to protect the privacy of individuals whose most intimate concerns are to be revealed in the newspaper, and "the legal, moral, and ethical restrictions imposed upon journalists within [a] school community" that includes adolescent subjects and readers. Finally, we conclude that the principal's decision to delete two pages of *Spectrum*, rather than to delete only the offending articles or to require that they be modified, was reasonable under the circumstances as he understood them. Accordingly, no violation of First Amendment rights occurred.

The judgment of the Court of Appeals for the Eighth Circuit is therefore reversed.

"*The decision was a resounding victory for school administrators and a defeat for student journalists.*"

The *Hazelwood* Decision Resulted in a Loss of First Amendment Rights for Public School Students

David Hudson

In the following viewpoint Cathy Kuhlmeier Cowan reflects on her role in Hazelwood School District et al. v. Kuhlmeier et al., *a landmark 1988 Supreme Court case. Cowan was one of three high school journalists who protested the principal's editing of newspaper content. The articles in question were about divorce and teen pregnancy and abortion, and school administrators felt the content was inappropriate and potentially libelous. The Supreme Court sided with the school administrators in ruling that the students' First Amendment rights had not been violated. Cowan tells* Freedom Forum *staff writer David Hudson that nearly fifteen years later she still believes that the school board and the Supreme Court were wrong. According to her, the Court's decision does impede the First Amendment rights of public school students.*

"Public school students don't have enough First Amendment rights," says Missouri native Cathy Cowan.

One might ask why Cowan's opinion on this subject should merit attention from anyone concerned with First Amendment rights. The reason: Cowan is the former Cathy Kuhlmeier, one of three former high school journalists who challenged the censorship of their school newspaper in a case that reached the United States Supreme Court.

Editing Objectionable Content

In the 1982–83 school year, Kuhlmeier was a student in the Journalism II class at Hazelwood East High School in St. Louis County, Mo. The class published the school newspaper, *The Spectrum.*

In April 1983, the class teacher and newspaper adviser Robert Stergos left the school to take a job in the private sector. Another teacher named Howard Emerson took his place.

At the time, a new edition of *The Spectrum* was almost ready. The paper was to include articles on teen pregnancy and the impact of divorce upon teen-agers. Emerson believed he needed the approval of the school principal, Robert Eugene Reynolds, before going to press.

Reynolds objected to the two articles. He said that the references to sexual activity and birth control were inappropriate in the teen-pregnancy article. He also said that the parents of a student named in the divorce story should have had an opportunity to voice their opinion in the article.

Reynolds deleted two pages of *The Spectrum.* The students, including Kuhlmeier—the layout editor—objected.

"A few of us contacted Mr. Stergos and he suggested we contact the American Civil Liberties Union," Cowan remembers. "We did and they told us we had a good case."

Marilyn Kuhlmeier left the decision about whether to pursue the matter entirely up to her daughter. She also supported her decision. "I absolutely supported her and believed that the school principal was wrong in censoring the articles. I was very proud of my daughter for fighting for her rights," she told freedomforum .org recently.

In the process, the three student journalists garnered several national awards for their commitment to the First Amendment. However, they did not prevail in the courts.

Filing Suit

Kuhlmeier and fellow *Spectrum* staffers Leslie Smart and Leann Tippett sued the Hazelwood School District and several school officials in federal court in 1984. They contended that the school district's actions in censoring their newspaper violated their First Amendment rights.

They argued that the school officials could not censor student expression unless they could reasonably forecast that the articles would cause a substantial disruption of school. They argued that the controlling case, supporting their view, was the Supreme Court's 1969 decision in *Tinker v. Des Moines Indep. Community School District*.

In *Tinker*, the high court ruled that school officials violated the First Amendment rights of several public school students by suspending them for wearing black armbands to school to protest U.S. involvement in the Vietnam War.

The district court rejected the Hazelwood students' claims, finding that school officials could restrict student speech in activities that are "an integral part of the school's educational function" such as a school-sponsored newspaper.

The district court also ruled in its 1985 opinion that the principal's actions were justified in order to show that the school did not support the "sexual norms of students" and to protect the privacy concerns raised by the articles.

Appealing the Ruling

In 1986, a three-judge panel of the 8th U.S. Circuit Court of Appeals reversed the district court. The appeals court ruled that

TEENS' VIEWS ON SCHOOL CENSORSHIP

Please indicate whether or not you think each of the following steps is an appropriate measure for public schools to take.

■ *Yes*   □ *No*

Restricting foul (bad) language in writing assignments

75%

25%

Placing limits on what students can write about in the school newspaper

45%

55%

Banning books, newspapers, and magazines considered by school officials to be offensive

44%

56%

Asked of US teens ages 13–17.

Taken from: Julie Ray, "Censorship: Do Teens Bow to School Control?" Gallup, July 12, 2005. www.gallup.com.

the school newspaper was a public forum "intended to be and operated as a conduit for student viewpoint."

The appeals court panel then determined that school officials could not censor the students' newspaper articles unless they could show that doing so was "necessary to avoid material and substantial interference with school work or discipline."

The school district appealed the decision to the United States Supreme Court. The district's attorney, Robert P. Baine Jr., says now that he was "certainly hopeful" that the school would prevail once the Supreme Court decided to hear the case.

"You never know if the court will take your case or how they will rule, but I knew that our chances were certainly raised when the Court agreed to hear the case," Baine recalls. "We felt that we had a good argument."

The school district and Baine were concerned about the composition of the court. At that time, former Chief Justice Warren Burger had retired. President Ronald Reagan had nominated Robert Bork for the high court, but the Senate had failed to

In the wake of the Hazelwood *ruling, student journalists can now be censored if school administrators perceive a potential disruption for the school.* © AP Images/Orlin Wagner.

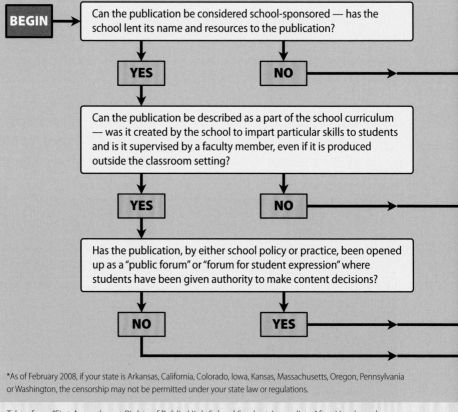

FIRST AMENDMENT RIGHTS OF PUBLIC HIGH SCHOOL STUDENT JOURNALISTS AFTER *HAZELWOOD SCHOOL DISTRICT V. KUHLMEIER*

This diagram describes how a court would determine if a particular act of censorship by school officials is legally permissible.

BEGIN → Can the publication be considered school-sponsored — has the school lent its name and resources to the publication?

YES

NO →

Can the publication be described as a part of the school curriculum — was it created by the school to impart particular skills to students and is it supervised by a faculty member, even if it is produced outside the classroom setting?

YES

NO →

Has the publication, by either school policy or practice, been opened up as a "public forum" or "forum for student expression" where students have been given authority to make content decisions?

NO

YES →

*As of February 2008, if your state is Arkansas, California, Colorado, Iowa, Kansas, Massachusetts, Oregon, Pennsylvania or Washington, the censorship may not be permitted under your state law or regulations.

Taken from: "First Amendment Rights of Public High School Student Journalists After *Hazelwood School District v. Kuhlmeier*," Student Press Law Center, 2008. www.splc.org.

confirm him. This left a Supreme Court with only eight justices rather than the customary nine.

"We were afraid of a court ruling 4–4," Baine said. If a higher court splits evenly, then the decision of the lower court stands. The 8th Circuit panel had ruled in favor of the students.

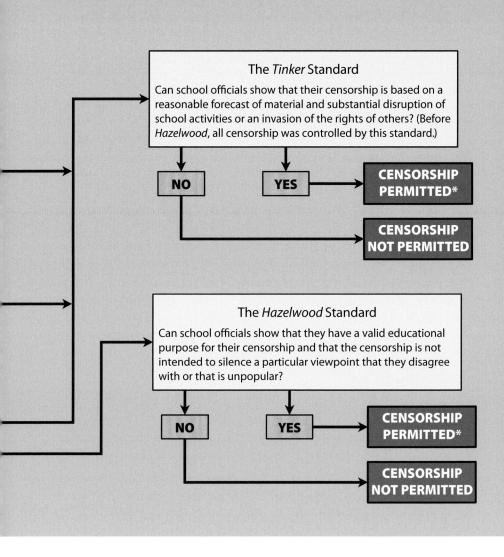

The school district pressed the argument that the school had greater authority over school-sponsored material and the curriculum. "The real issue in this case," Baine says, "is that the school paper produced as part of a class was a matter of the school curriculum."

"Ultimately, the board of education determined curricular content," Baine says. "The school can require a student newspaper to be reflective of good journalism standards."

Supreme Court Decision

In January 1988, the Supreme Court voted 5–3 in favor of the school in *Hazelwood School District v. Kuhlmeier.* In his majority opinion, Justice Byron White established a new standard for student speech that is school-sponsored. White wrote:

> ... we hold that educators do not offend the First Amendment by exercising editorial control over the style and content of student speech in school-sponsored expressive activities so long as their actions are reasonably related to legitimate pedagogical concerns.

In broad language, White reasoned that the school may censor student expression "that might reasonably be perceived to advocate drug or alcohol use, irresponsible sex . . . or to associate the school with any position other than neutrality on matters of political controversy."

Justice William Brennan, joined by Thurgood Marshall and Harry Blackmun, wrote a stinging dissenting opinion. Brennan wrote that "the case before us aptly illustrates how readily school officials (and courts) can camouflage viewpoint discrimination as the 'mere' protection of students from sensitive topics." Brennan accused the majority of approving of "brutal censorship."

He concluded: "The young men and women of Hazelwood East expected a civics lesson, but not the one the Court teaches them today."

Effect of the Ruling

The decision was a resounding victory for school administrators and a defeat for student journalists.

Baine says the court majority got the case right. "Again, this is an issue of the control of curriculum. I think that the *Tinker* case had been abused. The original basis for *Tinker* was good but some lower courts had expanded *Tinker* to the point where school officials would have had to permit the printing of anything students wrote."

"There is a saying that 'all education is local,' and I think the *Hazelwood* case stands for that principle," Baine says.

Mark Goodman, executive director of the Student Press Law Center, disputes many of Baine's points. "The case had nothing to do with what is being taught in the curriculum; it had solely to do with what students were allowed to publish," Goodman says.

Goodman believes that the Supreme Court should have continued to allow student journalism to be judged under the *Tinker* standard. "The school curriculum was not in danger under the *Tinker* standard," he says.

Even more disturbing, according to Goodman, is that "the legacy of *Hazelwood* is that it helped to create a generation of young people who don't have a clue what the First Amendment is about when they leave high school. Many students are taught that there is only freedom of expression when those in power agree with what you are saying."

Frank Susman, who helped argue the case on behalf of the students before the 8th Circuit but not before the Supreme Court, says that *Hazelwood* "was the start of the downfall for student First Amendment rights." He says the legacy of the case is that "school officials have acquired more and more power over students."

Unfortunate Results

By the time the Supreme Court had issued its opinion in 1988, Cathy Kuhlmeier was a senior at Southeast Missouri State, where she majored in advertising and commercial art.

She did not attend oral arguments because she says her attorney, Leslie Edwards, did not maintain sufficient contact with her. Sadly, she says the ordeal at Hazelwood left a "bad taste" in her mouth for journalism.

She married 10 years ago and has children. She teaches preschool in Missouri. She says she does not regret standing up to the school officials, even though she did not prevail.

And Cowan maintains that Principal Reynolds and the Supreme Court got the case wrong.

"I do feel that the legacy of the *Hazelwood* case is one of hurting student First Amendment rights. We should help students, and principals shouldn't be able to control everything," she says.

"I think we need to give students room to grow," she says. "Students need to be given the chance to do in-depth stories— more than just stories about the soccer game or who was named prom queen.

"I am a firm believer that you have a voice and that if you don't use your voice, things won't change," Cathy Cowan says today. "The neatest thing that happened to me recently was I got asked by the Indiana Press Association to come speak about the case. A girl came up to me after and said that I was a 'freedom fighter' and asked for my autograph.

"I never thought of myself as a freedom fighter, but I guess I did at least try to make a difference," Cowan says. "Students don't have enough First Amendment freedoms. There are a lot of very intelligent kids out there and we should listen to them more. Maybe if we did the world would be a better place."

> *"Title IX of the Education Act of 1972*
> *prohibits discrimination in educational*
> *institutions based on gender, marital,*
> *pregnancy or parenting status."*

Title IX Guarantees That Pregnant Teens Have the Right to an Education

Wendy C. Wolf

Wendy C. Wolf is the Founder and Senior Fellow of the Center for Assessment and Policy Development (CAPD). In the following viewpoint she argues that many teens are discriminated against in the school system because they are pregnant or have children. She asserts that Title IX protects pregnant teens and teen parents from being expelled, failed, or excluded from certain school activities. She outlines the many options that are available to pregnant or parenting teens, and she encourages young people to stand up for their right to an education.

On a daily basis and in many of the school districts that we have seen, many teens are discriminated against because of their pregnancy or parenting status:

Wendy C. Wolf, "Using Title IX to Protect the Rights of Pregnant and Parenting Teens," Center for Assessment and Policy Development, October 1999. Copyright © 1999 by Center for Assessment and Policy Development. All rights reserved. Reproduced by permission.

- They are forced into stand-alone alternatives which often lack educational instruction equivalent to their home school;

According to Title IX of the Education Act of 1972, it is illegal to force girls to stay out of school due to pregnancy. © Gage/Getty Images.

- They are not permitted to remain in or return to their home school;
- They are failed due to excessive absences because of the days missed due to the birth and/or illness of their child;
- They are required to stay out of school for a prescribed period of time; and
- They are restricted from certain courses (gym) and extracurricular activities (the Honor Society).

Furthermore, schools [sometimes] treat female teen parents quite differently than they do male teen parents: two examples include requiring young mothers to participate in parenting education [but] not requiring the same of young fathers and restricting certain activities of female teen parents [but] not of all teen fathers.

This is illegal. It violates the rights of pregnant and parenting teens protected under Title IX of the Education Act of 1972.

Title IX of the Education Act of 1972 prohibits discrimination in educational institutions based on gender, marital, pregnancy or parenting status. It clearly states that institutions receiving public funds cannot discriminate on the basis of these characteristics; it applies to programs affiliated with but not part of these institutions. It states that schools cannot require certain things of female teen parents if it does not require them of teen fathers. The law also requires schools to treat absences due to childbirth in the same way that it treats absences due to "other temporary disabilities."

Below, we review the implications of this law and its protections for: educational options and choices; parenting education; absence and leave policies; and extracurricular activities.

Educational Options

Students must be able to choose voluntarily their educational option: they cannot be forced into a stand-alone alternative school;

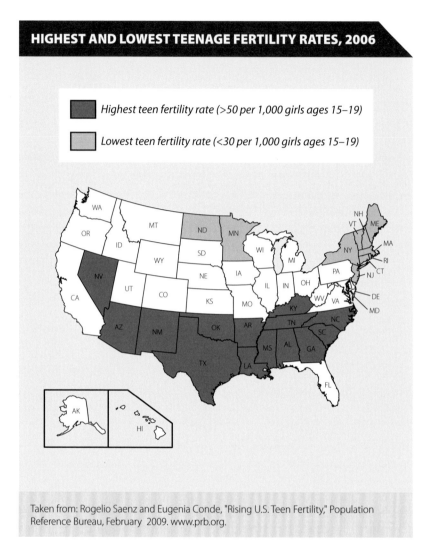

HIGHEST AND LOWEST TEENAGE FERTILITY RATES, 2006

Highest teen fertility rate (>50 per 1,000 girls ages 15–19)

Lowest teen fertility rate (<30 per 1,000 girls ages 15–19)

Taken from: Rogelio Saenz and Eugenia Conde, "Rising U.S. Teen Fertility," Population Reference Bureau, February 2009. www.prb.org.

they must be permitted to stay in their home school and be able to return to their home school at any time.

Stand-alone alternatives for teen parents must be of quality—the instructional program must be comparable to those offered in the comprehensive high school.

Schools cannot require parenting education of female teen parents if it does not do so for male teen parents.

Absences and Leave Policies

Schools cannot require students to be absent a prescribed period of time after the birth of their child.

If other students who miss school are entitled to make up assignments, so too are pregnant and parenting students.

If home instruction is available to others who are absent due to a medical condition, so too are pregnant and parenting teens entitled to such services.

Pregnant and parenting students cannot be penalized for absences due to childbirth. Students are permitted absences so long as they have a physician's note. If a district has a policy that students fail when they miss a proscribed number of days and they waive the policy for students with extended medical conditions or temporary disabilities, they must waive the policy for pregnant and parenting students so long as they have a note from a physician.

Extracurricular Activities

No restrictions can be placed on students because of pregnancy or parenting status.

No restrictions can be placed on participation in extracurricular activities: school personnel can only require notification from a physician to restrict participation in school activities if they require it from other students who see a doctor because of a health-related reason.

> *"Even though it's illegal, some public schools still pressure . . . pregnant teens to leave regular high schools for some kind of continuation school."*

Pregnant Teens Are Still Not Welcome in the Classroom

Allie Gottlieb

Allie Gottlieb is a former writer for Silicon Valley's Metroactive *newspaper. She works as a paralegal representing indigent death-row inmates in capital punishment cases in the state of California. In the following viewpoint Gottlieb argues that pregnant teenagers and teen parents are still being denied the right to a quality public school education despite Title IX's protection. They are often pushed into alternative schools, where the focus is on parenting instead of academics. Although some people assert that these alternative schools are better options for expecting teens, Gottlieb shares study results that indicate that denying pregnant teens the right to a mainstream education will only hurt them and will perpetuate a cycle of poverty and teen pregnancy.*

At 3:30 P.M., when school lets out for the day, two ponytailed Broadway High students sit waiting for their ride on the squat wall outside the school. Neither totes a backpack teeming with textbooks, term paper outlines or packets about upcoming SAT tests and college entrance data. But that doesn't mean their loads are light.

For instance, one of the girls is preoccupied with her 7-month-old son, who keeps spitting his blue pacifier onto the ground. "Could you pick that up for me?" she asks. "Sure," I say, and I do. The kid spits it out again.

The girls, both 16, say they get up at 6:30 every morning and catch two buses to get to the San Jose Unified School District's

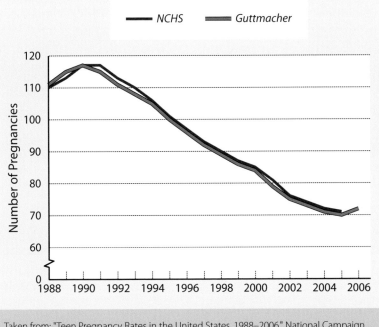

TEEN PREGNANCY RATES IN THE UNITED STATES, 1988–2006

This graph shows the teen pregnancy rate (per 1,000 girls ages 15–19) according to two data sources, the National Center for Heath Statistics (NCHS) and the Guttmacher Institute.

Taken from: "Teen Pregnancy Rates in the United States, 1988–2006," National Campaign to Prevent Teen and Unplanned Pregnancy, January 2010.

Broadway High School because "we got pregnant." They stop short of adding, "Duh!" But they explain that, on the advice of counselors and parents, the decision to leave their old schools to attend Broadway's Young Mothers/Young Families Program for pregnant and parenting teens, tucked beneath the Almaden Expressway, near Blossom Hill, was virtually automatic.

Even though it's illegal, some public schools still pressure—or force—pregnant teens to leave regular high schools for some kind of continuation school. A recent undercover study on high schools in Santa Clara County revealed that 25 percent of the time school officials act out age-old prejudices and policies against teenage sexuality. And the girls lose their legal right not only to an equal education but also to the goodies that go with it: college entrance assistance, advanced-placement classes and the experience of being at a high school with kids who aren't pregnant or being punished for school infractions.

"You can't come to our school" was how a Los Altos Union High School official succinctly put it to one teenage caller, who said she wanted to enroll at Los Altos and was pregnant. "Well, I really just want to go to regular school," the teen pressed. "Is there any way that I can go to a normal school?" The official said no. The caller later wrote: "She said that there was not [a possibility to attend a regular school], using the word 'honey' when she spoke to me."

Freedom of Choice

The answer from the administrator to this teen, as it turns out, was a lie. Alternative schools, such as the ones most pregnant girls are being sent to, are by law voluntary, a fact many girls don't seem to know. And furthermore, Title IX of the federal Education Amendments of 1972 and the California Education Code outlaw all forms of discrimination by public schools on the basis of sex, which can be applied to pregnant teens.

Despite the laws, six high schools in Santa Clara County were caught discriminating against pregnant teens in an undercover study conducted by San Francisco- and San Jose-based lawyers and [child] and gender-equality advocates who had heard complaints about local schools' treatment of pregnant teens.

The reports had been alarming. They heard, for instance, that one regular (also called comprehensive) school transferred a pregnant student to an alternative (also called continuation) school just days before graduation, ostensibly to spare the school the embarrassment of having a pregnant girl stroll across the stage in cap and gown before hundreds of onlookers. They received another report that a school counselor told the student body president, who was pregnant, that she was a bad role model and should resign her post.

Citing these examples, the Public Interest Law Firm, Legal Advocates for Children & Youth, Equal Rights Advocates and Fenwick & West LLP went to work investigating all Santa Clara County high schools, concluding with the January [2003] release of a 28-page document called "A Report on the Denial of Educational Opportunities for Pregnant Teens in Santa Clara County."

Gauging Reactions from California High School Officials

Testers posing as pregnant teens intending to move to a new school district phoned 24 high schools in Santa Clara County to check the school officials' reactions to a pregnant student wishing to enroll. The testers read from a basic script, pretending to be three months pregnant and about to move from Oakland to the district they were calling.

The testers were directed to say they want to attend a "normal" school rather than an alternative program or independent study. They were instructed to speak with officials as high up in the hierarchy as they could get and to log the conversations. The

Image on following page: Despite the law, many schools still pressure or force pregnant teens to leave their regular schools. © Ricki Rosen/Corbis SABA.

results single out Mountain View's Los Altos and Alta Vista high schools, Campbell's Westmont High School, Fremont's Lynbrook High School, Gilroy High School and San Jose High Academy as the offending schools, "which prohibited 'pregnant teen' tester from enrolling or strongly discouraged her."

The tester's call to San Jose High Academy went like this. The caller read the script, telling the school respondent she wanted enrollment information and was pregnant. The respondent told the tester she would give her the number for Broadway's Young Mothers/Young Families Program. The tester said, "I just want to go to a normal school." The respondent "paused and said that she has an embarrassing question to ask me: 'Does your tummy show yet?'"

When the tester said no, the school staffer said she could attend San Jose High Academy until she started showing and then should transfer to Broadway.

The January [2003] report outlines some of the same concerns that the Broadway students [mentioned earlier] raised. The 16-year-old mother of the 7-month-old regrets giving up dance classes, playing the clarinet in band and eating lunch in a cafeteria with her friends, all things that are lacking at Broadway. Overall, schools like Broadway are "inferior to mainstream high schools," the report states. It cites "fewer curriculum options such as electives and advanced classes," fewer athletic programs, shorter days and environments that aren't conducive to learning. . . .

A Cycle of Poverty

Studies repeatedly show . . . that insufficient education helps perpetuate the cycle of poverty and teen pregnancy. In 1998, for example, a teen-parent focus group formed at Foothill High School on San Jose's East Side determined that young parents come with a lot of unmet needs, a revelation that led to funding for the California School Age Families Education (Cal-SAFE) Program for pregnant and parenting teens, unveiled in 2000.

The "No Time for Complacency" report, which was released on March 17 [2003] by Berkeley's Public Health Institute, holds this to be true five years later. Teen moms "exhibit poorer psychological functioning, lower levels of educational attainment and high school completion, more single parenthood, and less stable employment," it reads.

"Because completing high school is essential to breaking the cycle of teen pregnancy and adult poverty, schools must ensure that pregnant and parenting teens have access to the full range of educational opportunities available to other students," reads a policy brief published by the California Women's Law Center.

Positive Aspects of Continuation Schools

Still others see the role of schools like Broadway as a necessary rescue operation for girls who weren't exactly on the college track to begin with. "The majority of students who come here haven't been in school for a while because of child care," says Esmeralda Rosales, who got pregnant at 17 and temporarily left her home school, Leland, for Broadway. Free child care was a big part of her choice to attend Broadway. She continued to use Broadway's child care service even after returning to Leland to graduate with her friends. Rosales, now a 23-year-old office assistant at Broadway, notes that an inability to buy care for kids is a huge barrier for many teens with experiences similar to her own. As a result, she says, "Not everybody who gets pregnant stays in school."

Barbara Rodriguez, who runs Broadway's Young Mothers Program, became a teen mother in the '60s and met with an even less receptive society. "It was scary," she recalls. "As a teenager, you feel it isn't going to happen to you."

She dropped out of school, and it took her 20 years to finish her education. Rodriguez believes that it is significant that the program at Broadway offers teenagers the help that she didn't have. "In some respects it's easier for girls now," she says. "When I was in high school, if a girl got pregnant, she left. . . . Now the girls have choices." . . .

Here and Now

San Jose Unified School District doesn't think it has a problem. In response to the report that accuses its school officials of breaking the anti-discrimination laws, district director Michael K. Carr wrote a letter to San Jose's Public Interest Law Firm blaming a temp for violating the rules at San Jose High Academy.

"I have reviewed your letter and packet of information and was dismayed that one of our substitute employees would have responded to a student's request in an inappropriate manner," he wrote. He then went on to say that he's working with the state Department of Education and the Educational Services Department to make sure the district has all the training it needs to avoid discriminating.

Of course, access to all schools is only part of the issue raised in the discrimination report. The other issue is equality between schools.

Access to Comprehensive Programs Is Vital

"I'd like to see the girls having the opportunity, as they do under the law, but in practice, to stay at their home school and have day care at their home school," California Law Center attorney [Nancy] Solomon says. "In conjunction [with] that, I would like to see pregnant and parenting teen programs be comparable [to mainstream schools]. The law requires them to be comparable. What I see is not comparable."

Attorney and study co-author [Erin] Scott adds that "in a perfect world," public schools "would be something more like the Cupertino High School model. There is a separate program, but it's right there on campus. The girls can take whatever classes they want. Something more like that is the solution."

In fact, Cupertino is a comprehensive high school complete with advanced-placement classes, parenting classes and child care. "It's not like once you're pregnant, oh my God, you're branded and you have to go to the parenting program," says principal Diane Burbank. As Burbank describes its enrollment process, district residency is the most important entrance criterion.

The 16-year-old mom from Broadway High School who takes two buses every morning to school might like the option of staying in her own district. It sounds like she would consider it.

"I would love to go to a regular high school," she says. "Because at a regular high school, you learn more. And there are more activities like sports and dancing. I used to be in a dancing class. I liked that. But at Broadway, we don't have that opportunity. We have PE, but we wear the same clothes as we wear during the day."

| "Abstinence-only-until-marriage
| programs jeopardize the health of
| sexually active teens. . . ."

Abstinence-Only Sex Education Programs Violate Teens' Rights

American Civil Liberties Union

In the following viewpoint the American Civil Liberties Union (ACLU), a group that fosters the civil rights of all Americans, argues that sex education programs that dictate abstinence only until marriage are not effective and compromise the rights of students. The authors explain that by teaching abstinence only, educators do not provide students with adequate information to make responsible decisions about sex. In addition, abstinence-only programs may jeopardize teen health by distributing inaccurate information and censoring other facts that would help students make healthier choices. The ACLU also insists that these programs create a negative environment for lesbian and gay teens and encourage troubling gender stereotypes. Finally, the ACLU objects to abstinence-only programs being paid for with taxpayers dollars because in many cases the programs espouse religious viewpoints.

Evidence shows that stressing the importance of waiting to have sex while providing accurate, age-appropriate, and complete information about how to use contraceptives can help teens delay sex and reduce sexual risk taking. Yet there is currently no federal program dedicated to supporting this approach. Instead, since 1996, the federal government has funneled more than a billion dollars into abstinence-only-until-marriage programming, even in the face of clear evidence that these programs do not work.

In addition to censoring vital health care information, abstinence-only-until-marriage programs raise other serious civil liberties concerns: They create a hostile environment for gay and lesbian teens; reinforce gender stereotypes; and in some instances use taxpayer dollars to promote one religious perspective.

Below is an in-depth discussion of the problems raised by federal abstinence-only-until-marriage programs.

Abstinence Programs Censor Vital Health Care Information

Currently, there are three federal programs dedicated to funding abstinence-only-until-marriage programs. Each requires eligible grantees to censor critical information that teens need to make healthy and responsible life decisions.

To receive funds under any of the federal programs, grantees must offer curricula that have as their "exclusive purpose" teaching the benefits of abstinence. In addition, recipients of abstinence-only-until-marriage dollars may not advocate contraceptive use or teach contraceptive methods except to emphasize their failure rates. Thus, recipients of federal abstinence-only-until-marriage funds operate under a gag order that censors vitally needed information. Grantees are forced either to omit any mention of topics such as contraception, abortion, homosexuality, and AIDS or to present these subjects in an incomplete and thus inaccurate fashion.

A church group promotes celibacy for teens. The ACLU contends that similar programs in schools violate some teens' rights. © Ian Waldie/Getty Images.

Research Shows that Abstinence Programs Don't Work

A rigorous, multi-year, scientific evaluation authorized by Congress and released in April 2007 presents clear evidence that abstinence-only-until-marriage programs don't work. The study by Mathematica Policy Research, Inc., which looked at four federally funded programs and studied more than 2,000 students, found that abstinence-only program participants were just as likely to have sex before marriage as teens who did not participate. Furthermore, program participants had first intercourse at the same mean age and the same number of sexual partners as teens who did not participate in the federally funded programs.

In addition, an academic study of virginity pledge programs—which encourage students to make a pledge to abstain from sex until marriage and are often a component of abstinence-only-until-marriage curricula—found that while in limited circumstances virginity-pledgers may delay first intercourse, they still have sex before marriage and are less likely than non-pledgers to use contraception at first intercourse and to get tested for STDs [sexually transmitted diseases] when they become sexually active.

On the other hand, there is ample evidence that programs that include information about both waiting to have sex and effective contraceptive use can help delay sex and reduce sexual risk taking among teens. Many of these programs have been shown to significantly delay the initiation of sex, reduce the frequency of sex, reduce the number of sexual partners, and increase condom or contraceptive use among sexually active teens. Research also shows that sex education curricula that discuss contraception—by presenting accurate information about contraceptive options, effectiveness, and use—do not increase sexual activity.

Abstinence Programs Withhold Information Teens Need

Abstinence-only-until-marriage programs are increasingly replacing other forms of sex education in schools. Between 1995 and 2002, "[t]he proportion of adolescents who had received any formal instruction about methods of birth control declined significantly," and by 2002, one-third of adolescents had not received any instruction on contraception. At the same time, in 1999, 23 percent of secondary school sexuality education teachers taught abstinence as the only way of avoiding STDs and pregnancy, up from 2 percent in 1988. When abstinence-only-until-marriage programs do present information about pregnancy prevention and testing and treatment of STDs, they do so incompletely and/or inaccurately. For example, a 2004 congressional report concluded that many federally funded abstinence-only-until-marriage curricula "misrepresent the effectiveness of condoms in preventing sexually transmitted diseases and pregnancy" by exaggerating their failure rates.

STATE-SPECIFIC TEENAGE BIRTH RATES

This map shows teenage birth rates for 15–19 year olds by state, 2008.

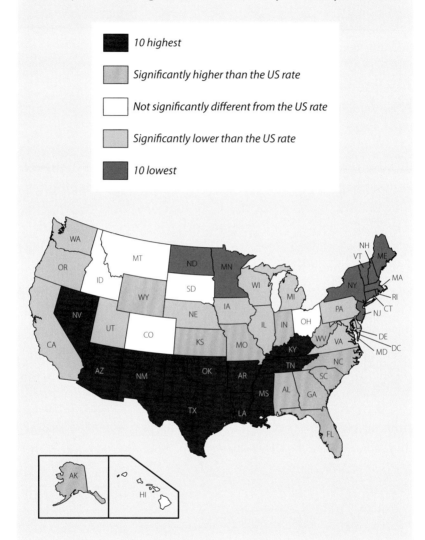

10 highest

Significantly higher than the US rate

Not significantly different from the US rate

Significantly lower than the US rate

10 lowest

US rate was 41.5 per 1,000 women aged 15–19 years.

Taken from: T.J. Mathews, Paul D. Sutton, Brady E. Hamilton, and Stephanie J. Ventura, "State Disparities in Teenage Birth Rates in the United States," *NCHS Data Brief*, October 2010.

We need to help teenagers make healthy and responsible life decisions by giving them full and accurate information about the transmission and treatment of STDs, and how to use contraception effectively. Abstinence-only-until-marriage programs jeopardize the health of sexually active teens and leave those who become sexually active unprepared.

Abstinence Programs Create a Hostile Environment for Lesbian and Gay Teens

Many abstinence-only-until-marriage programs use curricula that discriminate against gay and lesbian students and stigmatize homosexuality. The federal guidelines governing these programs state that they must teach that a "mutually faithful monogamous relationship in [the] context of marriage is the expected standard of human sexual activity." In a society that generally prohibits gays and lesbians from marrying, such a message rejects the idea of sexual intimacy for lesbians and gays and ignores their need for critical information about protecting themselves from STDs in same-sex relationships.

A review of the leading abstinence-only-until-marriage curricula found that most address same-sex sexual behavior only within the context of promiscuity and disease, and several are overtly hostile to lesbians and gay men. For example, materials from an abstinence-only-until-marriage program used recently in Alabama include the following: "[S]ame sex 'unions' cannot provide an adequate means of achieving a genuine physical relationship with another human being because this type of 'union' is contrary to the laws of nature."

By talking only about sex within marriage and teaching about STDs as a form of moral punishment for homosexuality, abstinence-only-until-marriage programs not only undermine efforts to educate teens about protecting their health, [they also] create a hostile learning environment for lesbian and gay students and the children of lesbian and gay and/or single parents.

Many Abstinence Programs Feature Harmful Gender Stereotypes

In addition to featuring false and misleading information, many abstinence-only-until-marriage programs present stereotypes about men and women as scientific facts. In an attempt to demonstrate differences between men and women, one popular program, WAIT Training, instructs teachers to "[b]ring to class frozen waffles and a bowl of spaghetti noodles without sauce. Using these as visual aids, explain how research has found that men's brains are more like the waffle, in that their design enables them to more easily compartmentalize information. Women's minds, on the other hand, are interrelated due to increased brain connectors." Similarly, the teacher's manual for Why Know Abstinence Education Programs suggests that girls are responsible for boys' inability to control their sexual urges: "One subtle form of pressure can be the way in which a girl acts toward her boyfriend. If the girlfriend is constantly touching him and pressing against him, or wearing clothing which is tight or revealing of her body, this will cause the guy to think more about her body than her person, and he may be incited toward more sexual thoughts."

Many abstinence-only-until-marriage programs are riddled with similarly troubling discussions of gender. Such stereotypes and false information undermine women's equality and promote an outmoded and discredited view of women's and men's roles and abilities.

Some Abstinence Programs Use Taxpayer Dollars to Promote One Religious Perspective

Although the U.S. Constitution guarantees that the government will neither promote nor interfere with religious belief, some abstinence-only-until-marriage grantees violate this core freedom by using public dollars to convey overt religious messages or to impose religious viewpoints. The ACLU has successfully challenged this misuse of taxpayer dollars:

In May 2005, the ACLU filed a lawsuit challenging the federally funded promotion of religion by a nationwide abstinence-only-until-marriage program called the Silver Ring Thing. The program was rife with religion. In its own words, "The mission of Silver Ring is to saturate the United States with a generation of young people who have taken a vow of sexual abstinence until marriage. . . . This mission can only be achieved by offering a personal relationship with Jesus Christ as the best way to live a sexually pure life." The lawsuit, *ACLU of Massachusetts v. Leavitt*, brought swift results: In August 2005, the U.S. Department of Health and Human Services (HHS) suspended the Silver Ring Thing's funding, pending corrective or other action. And in February 2006, the parties reached a settlement in which HHS agreed that any future funding would be contingent on the Silver Ring Thing's compliance with federal law prohibiting the use of federal funds to support religious activities. Soon after, HHS released new guidelines for all abstinence-only-until-marriage grantees to ensure that government funds will not be used to promote religion. These guidelines were modeled after the settlement agreement in *ACLU of Massachusetts v. Leavitt*.

In 2002, the ACLU challenged the use of taxpayer dollars to support religious activities in the Louisiana Governor's Program on Abstinence (GPA), a program run on federal and state funds. Over the course of several years, the GPA had funded programs that, among other things, presented "Christ-centered" theater skits, held a religious youth revival, and produced radio shows that "share abstinence as part of the gospel message." In violation of the Constitution, a federal district court found that GPA funds were being used to convey religious messages and advance religion. The court ordered Louisiana officials to stop this misuse of taxpayer dollars. The case was on appeal when the parties settled. The GPA agreed to closely monitor the activities of the programs it funds and to stop using GPA dollars to "convey religious messages or otherwise advance religion in any way."

Major Groups Support Comprehensive Sexuality Education

The vast majority of U.S. parents, teachers, and leading medical groups believe that teens should receive complete and accurate information about delaying sexual activity and contraception.

In a nationwide poll conducted in 2004 for the Kaiser Family Foundation, National Public Radio, and the Kennedy School of Government, researchers found that an overwhelming majority of parents want sex education curricula to cover topics such as abortion and sexual orientation, as well as how to use and where to get contraceptives, including condoms.

A 1999 nationally representative survey of 7th–12th grade teachers in the five specialties most often responsible for sex education found that a strong majority believed that sexuality education courses should cover birth control methods (93.4%), factual information about abortion (89%), where to go for birth control (88.8%), the correct way to use a condom (82%), and sexual orientation (77.8%), among other topics.

Similarly, major medical organizations have advocated for and/or endorsed comprehensive sexuality education, including the American Medical Association, the American Academy of Pediatrics, the American College of Obstetrics and Gynecology, and the Society for Adolescent Medicine.

Organizations to Contact

The editors have compiled the following list of organizations concerned with the issues debated in this book. The descriptions are derived from materials provided by the organizations.

Alliance Defense Fund (ADF)

15100 North 90th Street, Scottsdale, AZ 85260
(800) TELL-ADF • fax: (480) 444-0025
website: www.alliancedefensefund.org

The ADF is a legal alliance defending the right to hear and speak about Christian beliefs through the legal defense and advocacy of religious freedom, the sanctity of human life, and traditional family values. The organization asserts that parents have the job of educating their children about sex, and it defends the right of parents to opt their children out of sex education classes. In addition to position statements supporting these rights, the ADF website functions as a clearinghouse of news regarding sex education.

American Civil Liberties Union (ACLU)

915 15th Street NW, Washington, DC 20005
(202) 393-4930 • fax: (757) 563-1655
e-mail: wso@al-anon.org
website: www.aclu.org

The ACLU is a national organization that works to defend Americans' civil rights as guaranteed by the US Constitution. It opposes federal funding for abstinence-only sex education by arguing that such instruction violates the civil rights and the freedom of speech of students and teachers. Among the ACLU's numerous publications are "Responsible Spending: Real Sex Ed for Real Lives," "Helping Teens Make Healthy and Responsible

Decisions about Sex," and "Abstinence-Only Education Fact Sheet."

Americans for a Society Free from Ageism (ASFAR)

PO Box 11358, Chicago, IL 60611-0358
e-mail: editor@asfar.org
website: asfar.org

Americans for a Society Free from Ageism (ASFAR) was founded in 1996 to combat age-based restrictions of the basic rights of all Americans, including access to an equal education. ASFAR educates the public on these core issues, and it has assisted in bringing student rights cases to court. The ASFAR website provides many publications, including position papers on educational freedom and freedom of speech.

Child's Rights Information Network (CRIN)

East Studio, 2, Pontypool Place, London, SE1 8QF, United Kingdom
+44 20 7401 2257
e-mail: info@crin.org
website: www.crin.org

Inspired by the United Nations Convention on the Rights of the Child, CRIN is building a global network for children's rights. Through advocacy campaigns and international children's rights coalitions, CRIN strives to make existing human rights enforcement mechanisms accessible for all. The CRIN website provides information about children's rights in countries across the globe and provides access to their investigative reports, including "Children in Haiti—One Year After" and "Realizing Children's Rights."

The Freechild Project

PO Box 6185, Olympia, WA 98507-6185
(360) 489-9680

e-mail: info@freechild.org
website: www.freechild.org

The mission of the Freechild Project is to advocate, inform, and celebrate social change led by and with young people around the world, especially those who have been historically denied the right to participate. One of the main focuses of the Freechild Project is education, including student rights to homeschooling, unschooling, and education advocates. The group's website contains a number of publications, including *Guide to Social Change Led By and With Young People* and *Guide to Cooperative Games for Social Change.*

The Gay and Lesbian Alliance Against Defamation (GLAAD)

5455 Wilshire Boulevard, #1500, Los Angeles, CA 90036
(323) 933-2240 • Fax: (323) 933-2241
website: www.glaad.org

GLAAD amplifies the voice of the LGBT (lesbian, gay, bisexual, and transgender) community by empowering real people to share their stories, holding the media accountable for the words and images they present, and helping grassroots organizations communicate effectively. By ensuring that the stories of LGBT people are heard through the media, GLAAD promotes understanding, increases acceptance, and advances equality. In addition to position papers, GLAAD's website offers several media guides, including *GLAAD College Media Reference Guide* for college journalists who wish to write about LGBT issues.

International Disability Alliance (IDA)

WCC Building, nos. 153–154, 150 route de Ferney, 1211 Genève
website: www.internationaldisabilityalliance.org

Established in 1999, the International Disability Alliance (IDA) is the network of global and regional organizations of persons with disabilities (DPOs) promoting the effective implementation of the UN Convention on the Rights of Persons with Disabilities. IDA was instrumental in establishing the International Disability Caucus (IDC), the network of global, regional and national organizations of persons with disabilities and allied nongovernmental organizations. The IDA publishes the *Disability Rights Bulletin*.

National Youth Rights Association (NYRA)

1101 15th Street NW, Suite 200, Washington, DC 20005
(202) 835-1739
website: www.youthrights.org

The National Youth Rights Association (NYRA) defends the civil and human rights of young people in the United States by educating people about youth rights and empowering young people to work on their own behalf in defense of their rights. NYRA believes that certain basic rights are intrinsic parts of American citizenship and transcend age or status limits. In addition to annual reports, NYRA's website provides access to its statements, including "Drinking Age" and "Curfew."

Parents and Students for Academic Freedom (PSAF)

1015 15th Street NW, Suite 900, Washington, DC 20005
(202) 969-2467
e-mail: sara@studentsforacademicfreedom.org
website: www.psaf.org

Parents and Students for Academic Freedom (PSAF) is a subgroup of Students for Academic Freedom (SAF), which is a clearinghouse of information for parents, students, and educators. PSAF provides information for individuals who feel that the education their public schools provide is biased or in violation of student rights. Some of their available publications include "Academic Freedom Code for K-12 Schools" and "The Indoctrination of America's Youth."

SoundOut

PO Box 6185, Olympia, WA 98507
e-mail: info@soundout.org
website: www.soundout.org

SoundOut is an expert assistance program focused on promoting student voices and meaningful student involvement throughout education. SoundOut provides advocacy training for students and educators throughout the United States and Canada. In addition to providing a library of student resources, the SoundOut website provides access to its own publications, including "The Basics of Student Voice" and "Meaningful Student Involvement."

Student Press Law Center (SPLC)

1101 Wilson Blvd., Suite 1100, Arlington, VA 22209-2275
(703) 807-1904
website: www.splc.org

Founded in 1974, the Student Press Law Center (SPLC) has served high school and college journalists by educating them about their First Amendment rights. In addition, the SPLC offers free legal advice and attorney referrals to student journalists in need of assistance. In addition to FAQ sheets, the SPLC website offers a law library focused on student rights and a legal guide to relevant Supreme Court cases.

UNICEF

United States Fund for UNICEF, 125 Maiden Lane, 11th Floor, New York, NY 10038
(212) 686-5522 • Fax: (212) 779-1679
website: www.unicef.org

Mandated by the United Nations General Assembly, UNICEF is an international organization developed to support the needs of children, including access to education. In addition to serving as advocates for the world's most needy, UNICEF works with legislatures to shape global policies involving equality and compassion for children. In addition to the Annual Report, UNICEF also regularly publishes the *State of the World's Children* and *Progress for Children.*

For Further Reading

Books

Kern Alexander and M. David Alexander, *American Public School Law*. 7th ed. Belmont, CA: Wadsworth, 2009.

Stuart Biegel, *The Right to Be Out: Sexual Orientation and Gender Identity in America's Public Schools*. Minneapolis, MN: University of Minnesota Press, 2010.

Nelda H. Cambron-McCabe et al., *Legal Rights of Teachers and Students*. Boston: Pearson, 2009.

Kenneth Dautrich, *The Future of the First Amendment: The Digital Media, Civic Education, and Free Expression Rights in America's High Schools*. Lanham, MD: Rowman and Littlefield, 2008.

Anne Proffitt Dupre, *Speaking Up: The Unintended Costs of Free Speech in Public Schools*. Cambridge, MA: Harvard University Press, 2009.

James C. Foster, *BONG HiTS 4 JESUS: A Perfect Constitutional Storm in Alaska's Capital*. Fairbanks: University of Alaska Press, 2010.

David L. Hudson Jr., *Rights of Students*. New York: Chelsea House, 2011.

Jamin B. Raskin, *We the Students: Supreme Court Cases for and About Students*. Washington, DC: CQ Press, 2008.

Charles J. Russo et al., eds., *The Educational Rights of Students: International Perspectives on Demystifying the Legal Issues*. Lanham, MD: Rowman and Littlefield, 2007.

John A. Stokes, *Students on Strike: Jim Crow, Civil Rights, Brown, and Me: A Memoir*. Washington, DC: National Geographic, 2008.

Periodicals and Internet Sources

American Civil Liberties Union, "Know Your Prom Night Rights! A Quick Guide for LGBT High School Students," www.aclu.org, April 11, 2011.

Boston College Law Review, "Parents, Students, and the Pledge of Allegiance: Why Courts Must Protect the Marketplace of Student Ideas," vol. 52, no. 1, January 2011.

The Daily Orange, "Investigation of Student Blog Challenges First Amendment Rights," October 20, 2010.

Erica Frankenberg and Genevieve Siegel-Hawley, "Choice Without Equity: Charter School Segregation and the Need for Civil Rights Standards," *Education Digest*, vol. 76, no. 5, January 2011.

Kathy Luttrell Garcia, "Poison Pens, Intimidating Icons, and Worrisome Websites: Off-Campus Student Speech that Challenges Both Campus Safety and First Amendment Jurisprudence," *St. Thomas Law Review*, vol. 23, no. 1, 2010.

Sameer Hinduja and Justin W. Patcha, "High-Tech Cruelty," *Educational Leadership*, vol. 68, no. 5, February 2011.

Reynolds Holding, "Speaking Up for Themselves," *Time*, May 21, 2007.

Chris Joyner, "Judge: Lesbian Student's Rights Violated," USAToday.com, March 24, 2010.

Paria Kooklan, "Students Protecting Democracy," *Student Lawyer*, vol. 39, no. 2, October 2010.

Alexis Madrigal, "Creationism Dig Violated Student's Rights," *Wired Science*, wired.com, May 7, 2009.

Lloyd B. Minor, "From Desegregation to Diversity and Inclusion," *Vital Speeches of the Day*, vol. 77, no. 1, January 2011.

Abby Marie Mollen, "In Defense of the 'Hazardous Freedom' of Controversial Student Speech," *Northwestern University Law Review*, vol. 102, no. 3, Summer 2008.

Ron Schacter, "Power to the Students!" *District Administration*, vol. 46, no. 5, May 2010.

Joseph A. Tomain, "Cyberspace Is Outside the Schoolhouse Gate: Offensive, Online Student Speech Receives First Amendment Protection," *Drake Law Review*, vol. 59, no. 1, Fall 2010.

Emily Gold Waldman, "Students' Fourth Amendment Rights in Schools: Strip Searches, Drug Tests, and More," *Touro Law Review*, vol. 26, no. 4, June 2011.

Index